IMPROVISING Jazz Guitar.

Amsco Publications
New York/London/Sydney

from Joe

To the memory of my grandfather, Anthony Sofia, for his continued support and musical inspiration.

from Peter

To Professor Cohen, who—in my salad days when I was green in judgement, cold in blood—had a because for my every why.

Book design and layout by Len Vogler
Edited by Peter Pickow

Order No. AM 37326
US International Standard Book Number: 0.8256.2259.X

Exclusive Distributors:
Music Sales Corporation
257 Park Avenue South, New York, NY 10010 USA
Music Sales Limited
8/9 Frith Street, London W1V 5TZ England
Music Sales Pty. Limited
120 Rothschild Street, Rosebery, Sydney, NSW 2018, Australia

Printed in the United States of America by
Vicks Lithograph and Printing Corporation

Contents

Foreword

There are great advantages to knowing what you're doing with your instrument on a technical level. Being educated in music theory can help to expand creativity and awareness in expressing yourself on your ax. **Improvising Jazz Guitar** provides a great opportunity for a musician to learn the skills of modern jazz theory.

In my most formative stage of musical development, I found Joe Bell to be a fine private teacher. I feel that studying his book is equally beneficial.

Steve Vai

Preface

The way to discover a new area of music-making is to make music. Although that may seem to be rather obvious, you would never know it from the way most books on jazz guitar are written. This one is different. In this book you will explore ideas and ways to play that yield immediate results. The method is to apply the concepts as you learn them. This has two important advantages: You will ultimately understand each idea better and more fully and you will be developing elements of your own personal style within the jazz idiom right from the beginning.

Improvising Jazz Guitar is set up in such a way as to allow you to work at your own pace. Each chapter presents one main idea along with plenty of examples, sample progressions or solos, full explanation of the theoretical concepts involved, and suggestions to help you begin to apply the technique to your playing right away. There is no doubt that a lot, if not all, of the information presented will be new to you. Be patient and keep in mind that the book is designed to get you playing and understanding jazz as quickly as possible. Although it may sound trite it is nonetheless true to say that nothing worthwhile is easy. In other words, there's no such thing as a free lunch. To really play any kind of music well you have to work pretty hard and jazz is no exception.

If you do get bogged down at any point, try to seek out a player or group of players more advanced than you. Observing how a more advanced player utilizes improvisational tools can clear up many vagaries that we cannot via the printed page. Plus, you can't go swimming without getting your feet wet so jump in and jam.

Another word of advice to you as you go through this book: Don't get bogged down in the theory. Music theory is great in that it allows you to understand why things work and so enables you to make the most of your playing skills. For instance, a working knowledge of major scales makes understanding modal scales a snap. On the other hand, you will get a lot more mileage out of learning a one-octave pattern for a modal scale and creating a few simple solos than you will from being able to write one down on paper. This is the spirit in which this book is offered: The theory behind the techniques is here, the scale patterns and "rules" for using them are here, but the accent is on playing, creating, and enjoying your own music.

If You Can Play the Blues, You Can Start Playing Jazz

One of the first things any jazz improviser learns to have fun with is the blues, the ice-breaker at jam sessions since the beginning of improvised music. One thing that makes the blues such a common denominator is the deceptive simplicity of the chord progressions. You may already know that most blues progressions are made up of what are known as I, IV, and V chords. These numbers refer to degrees of the major scale.

In C:

I	II	III	IV	V	VI	VII	I
C	D	E	F	G	A	B	C

By substituting different chords for the ones usually used we can increase the tonal color and excitement of a standard blues progression to make it sound more like jazz.

Chords

Let's start out with this standard I IV V blues progression:

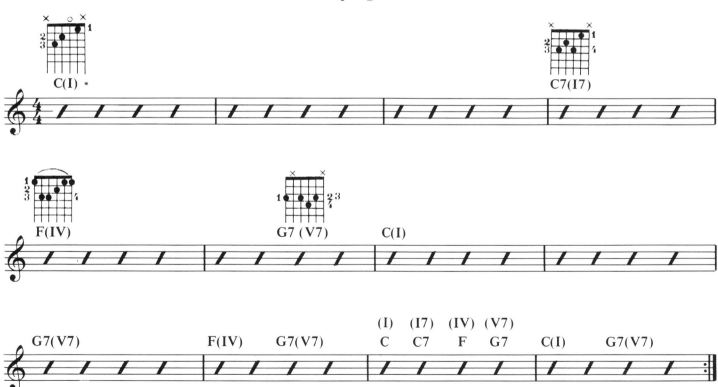

---

* Throughout this book you will find suggestions for chord voicings to use in playing each progression presented. If you know other ways to play the chords, feel free to experiment.

Each chord in this progression has its own distinct musical effect on the listener. Let's examine each chord a little closer. First of all, this progression begins and ends with a C chord. This is the I chord; think of it as home base. From the I we depart from a musical area that sounds "at rest" and enter musical areas that add tension and color to the sound. Finally we return to home base.

The I chord sounds so solid because it is made up of tones which we call *inactive* tones. The IV and V chords add tension to the progression because they introduce *active* tones. To get the idea of how active and inactive tones interact, try this simple example.

First play this open-position C chord on the middle four strings:

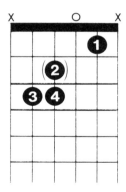

Now put your fourth finger down on the fourth string, third fret to play a C Suspended Fourth chord.

Notice how the F note you have added has caused tension in the sound. F is an active tone in the key of C. It is the fourth degree of the C major scale.

I	II	III	IV
C	D	E	F

Therefore, the complete F chord, F A C, because it has the F note in it, adds tension to the C blues progression.

Now let's look at the G7 chord. This chord moves even farther away from the home-base chord of C because it adds two additional active tones to the sound. These active tones are B and D (G7 = G B D F).

We are going to be making a lot of use of this concept of active and inactive tones and chords. As an example, let's try introducing a simple 'substitution' into our classic blues progression. Instead of F, the IV chord, play D Minor Seventh, the II−7 chord.

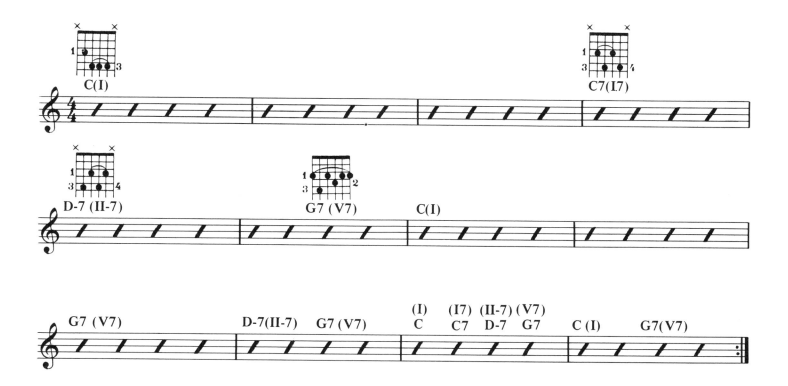

It sounds great, but why? The reason lies in the similarities between the F and the D−7. Let's take a closer look at the F, or IV, chord. This chord contains the notes F A C.

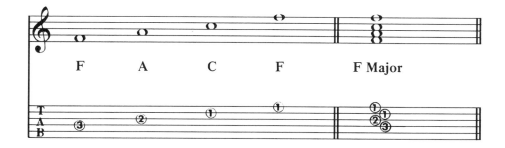

In the key of C, D Minor Seventh is the II chord and is made up of the notes D F A C; the same notes as the F chord with an additional D note at the bottom.

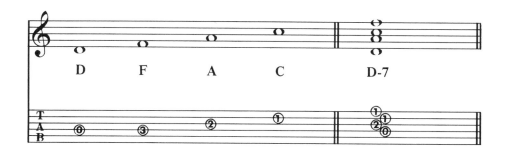

Because these two chords have three notes in common—especially the F, an active tone—the D Minor Seventh may replace the F chord in the C blues progression. We may now say that C F G7 = C D−7 G7 *or* I IV V7 = I II−7 V7.

Play the progression again and notice how the sequence II−7 V7 I sounds just as complete as IV V7 I only jazzier. This sequence (referred to as "two-five-one" or simply "two-five") is the most popular progression in jazz. The tunes "Giant Steps" by John Coltrane and "Tune-Up" by Miles Davis are examples of tunes which make extensive use of this chord sequence. When the II−7 goes to the V7 there is a real need for resolution to I. (This is usually what happens, although sometimes this I is minor and acts as the II−7 of another II V I sequence. More on this later.)

Here are a few more simple blues progressions utilizing II V I sequences to get you used to the sound. Play them with an ear to learning to recognize this all-important chord progression. Try to relate these simple examples to songs you know.

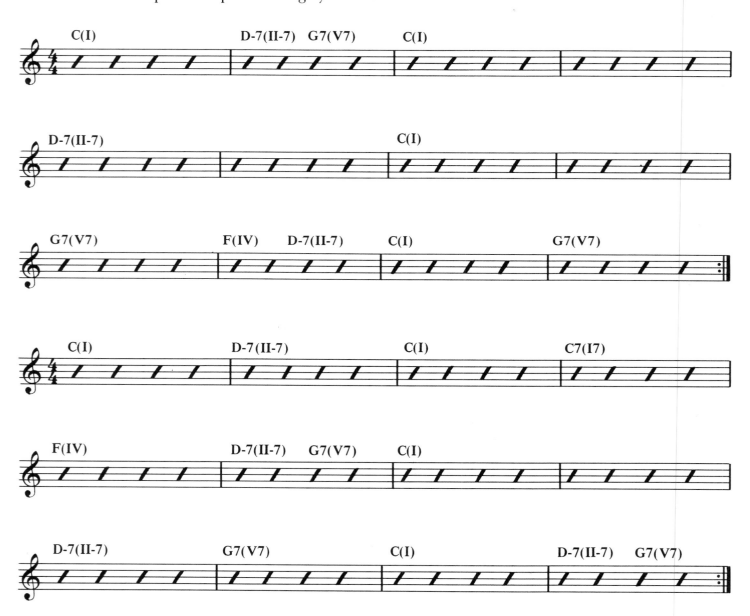

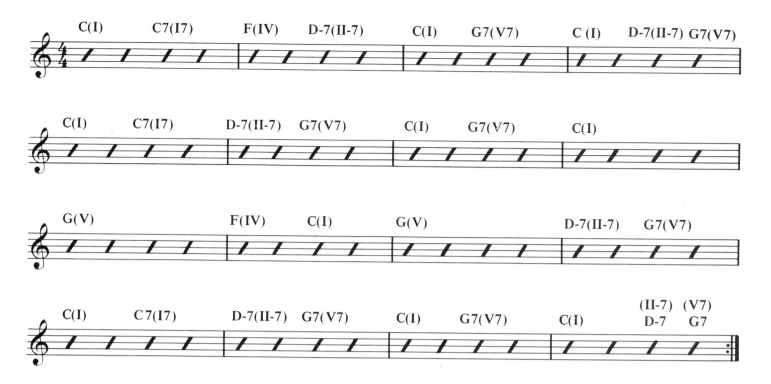

For more practice, try transposing these progressions to the keys indicated using the following sets of I, II−7, IV, and V7 chords.

Key of D

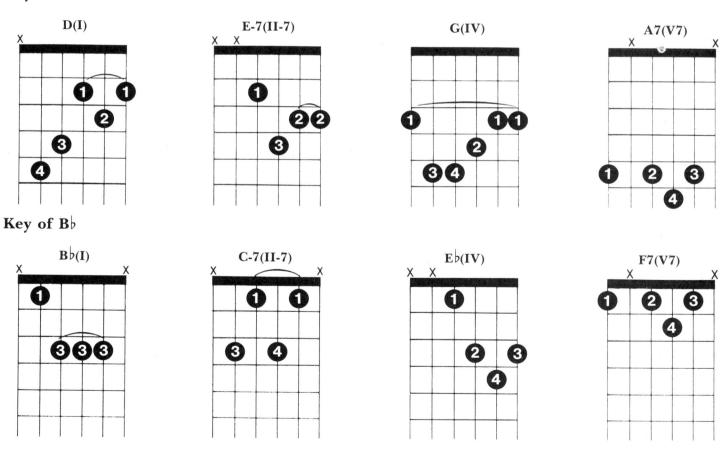

Key of B♭

Key of F

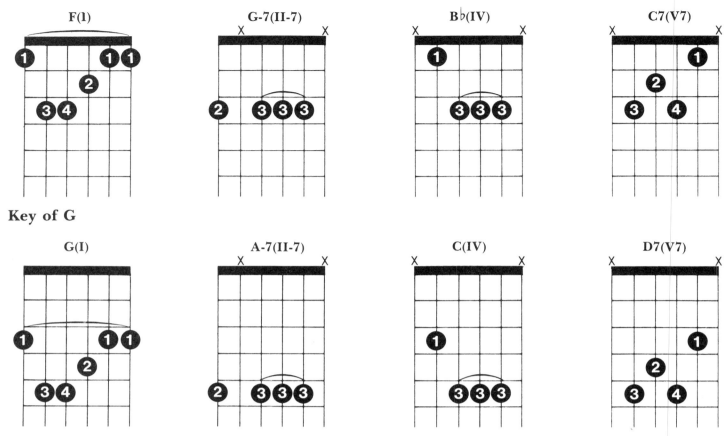

Key of G

If you play with a pick, use four downstrokes per measure. If you play fingerstyle, use thumb and three fingers to pinch the four strings of each chord four times per measure.

Melody

Now that you have an idea of how easy it is to jazz up a simple blues progression harmonically, let's try adding some melody. We will start by working with a major scale. The more you get into jazz, the more you realize the importance of scales. To start, here is a simple exercise.

First, play a C chord. Then slowly play the C major scale below.

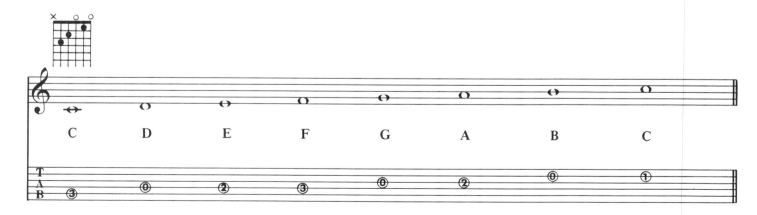

Take the time to listen to the chord, then slowly play the scale noticing how each note is affected by the sound first created by the C chord. If you can retain the sound of the C chord in your head, you should be able to hear that certain notes sound active, or tense, and add color to the C chord while others sound inactive and seem to blend into the sound. Here is the C scale again showing the active and inactive tones.

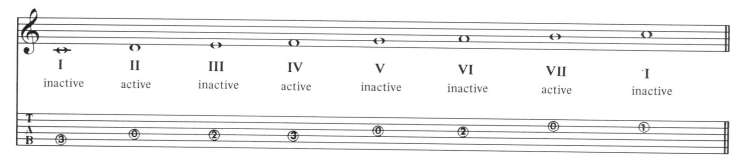

While you are thinking about this, try this eight-bar progression which makes use of the II V I sequence.

Now let's add a *head* (melody) to these changes. If you cannot get someone to play rhythm for you, just lay down the chord progression on tape and then play along with the recording. As you play the melody listen to how the active tones sound against the inactive chords. Also listen to the inactive tones against the active chords.

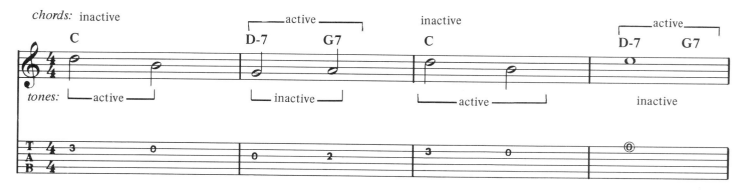

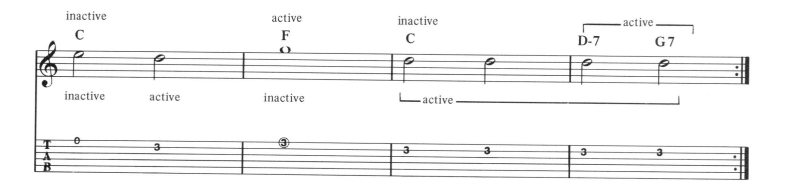

We can embellish this simple melody by adding a few extra notes and syncopating the rhythm.

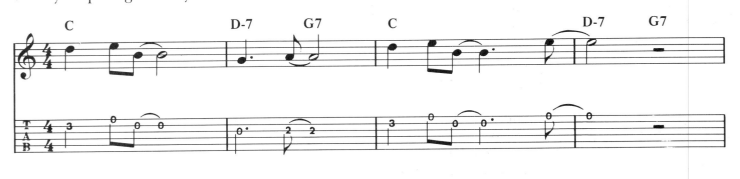

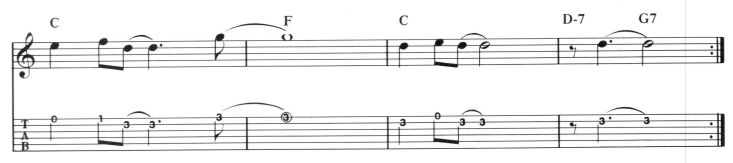

The careful and deliberate use of active and inactive tones is what gives jazz its various tonal colors. Try making up your own melodies using the C major scale against the following progressions. Use rhythmic variation and the active/inactive concepts discussed here to create your own style of improvisation. Remember: Always listen and try to be musical.

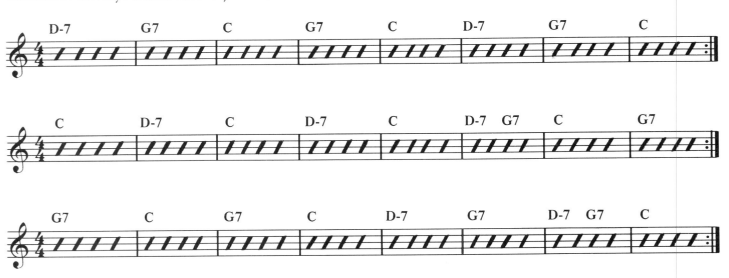

I hope that you were able to move right through this first chapter and are making good use of the ideas about chords and melody. It is important that you fully understand the concepts introduced as we are going to be developing and working with them throughout the rest of the book.

Something that you may want to consider at this point is starting your own "Riff Diary." As you experiment with the ideas in each chapter you are going to come up with certain riffs—both melodic and chordal—that you will want to remember. Actually writing these licks down in a notebook will give you valuable practice in transferring your ideas to paper but you may find it easier to record them on cassette. Either way, by taking a moment to make a note of each riff and the concept or situation to which it applies you will be creating a personal thesaurus of ideas to practice and work with.

Modal Jazz Is as Simple as Playing a Major Scale

There comes a time when all musicians, as their interest in jazz increases, hear about *modes*. Simply speaking, the modes are scales created through the displacement of the major scale. In other words, the major scale has a set arrangement of whole and half steps which may be conveniently altered by starting the scale on a degree other than I.

Below is a chart based on the key of C that will introduce you to the seven modes.

The Modes

Ionian   the "normal" major scale

Dorian   the minor scale built on the second degree of the major scale. Its characteristic tone, which distinguishes it from the 'natural minor' or 'Aeolian' scale (see below), is the raised VI.

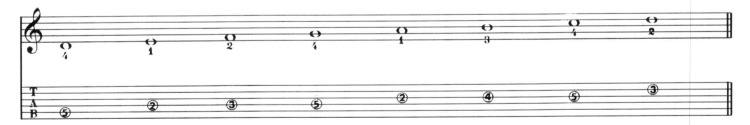

Phrygian   the minor scale built on the third degree of the major scale. Its Spanish flavor is due to its characteristic tone, the flat II.

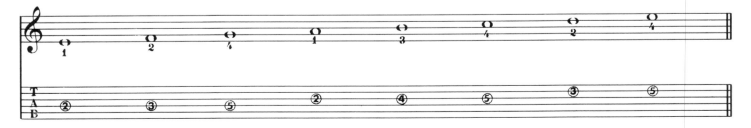

Lydian   a brighter major scale (with a raised IV) built on the
fourth degree of the major scale

Mixolydian   the major scale containing the dominant (flat) VII
built on the fifth degree of the major scale

Aeolian   the "normal" minor scale. Also known as the *relative* or
natural minor, it is built on the sixth degree of the
major scale.

Locrian   the minor scale containing a flat V and dominant (flat)
VII built on the seventh degree of the major scale

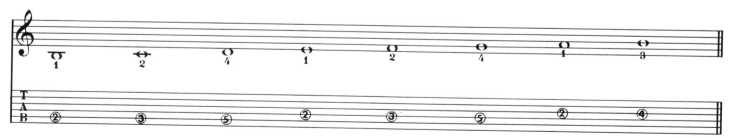

Here is a chart that demonstrates the interrelationships of the seven modes.

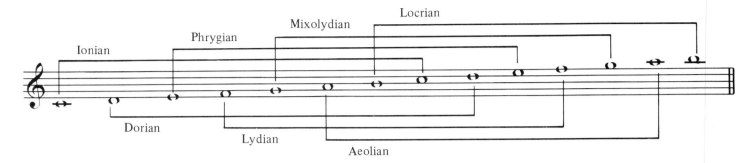

The Dorian Mode

Probably the most commonly used of these modes in jazz (with the exception of the Ionian, or major, scale) is the Dorian mode. The classic jazz example of Dorian-mode playing is "So What" by Miles Davis which moves back and forth between D Dorian and Eb Dorian. Another good example is the guitar solo from the Beatles' "Taxman."

Here is a chance for you to play a few Dorian-mode scales. Have someone play this chord progression while you play the melody which is based on the scales that correspond to each chord. Start out slowly and try to be accurate with the rhythms as notated. Using a metronome or rhythm box to set the tempo might help.

chord	scale
D−7	D Dorian (C major scale from D to D)
C−7	C Dorian (Bb major scale from C to C)
Bb−7	Bb Dorian (Ab major scale from Bb to Bb)

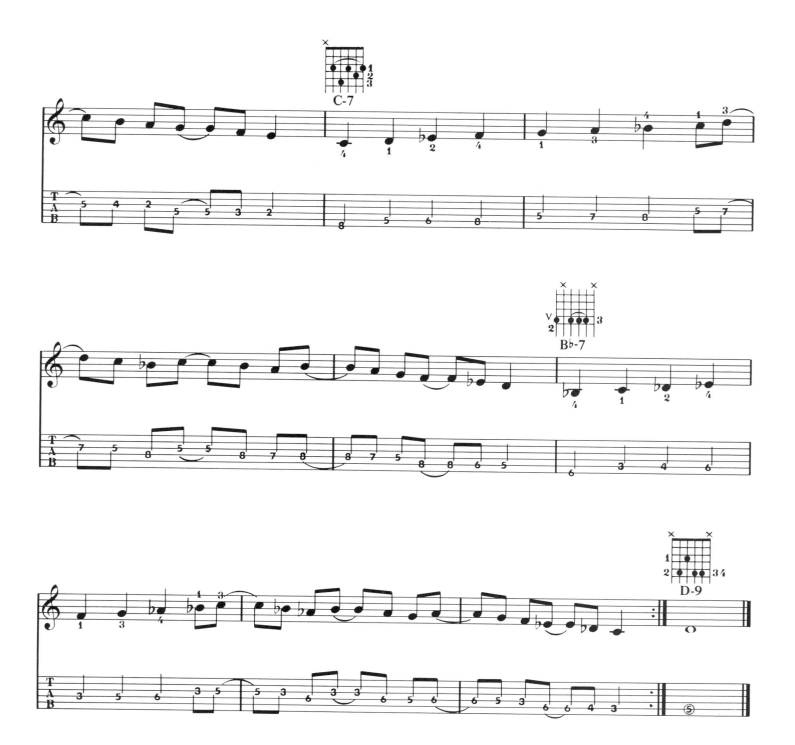

Notice that the fingerings for all three scales in the example above are identical even though the D Dorian scale starts on the fifth string while the other two begin on the sixth. Here is a diagram summarizing these scale patterns to help you learn them.

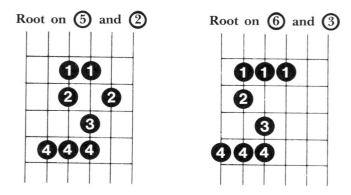

As you get familiar with the sound and feel of these scales, make sure that you are trying to play musically. In fact, you should always try to bring something from your own personality to every musical situation.

Let's play through another example of modal jazz. Here is a progression that is slightly more complex than the one you have just played.

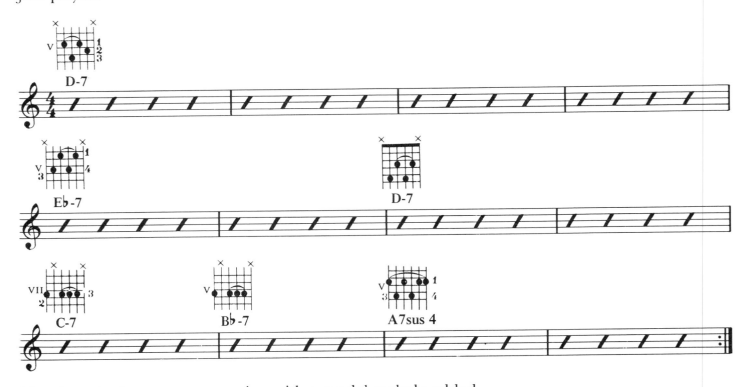

Now here is the same progression with a modal melody added. Take note of which scales are used in this head and then use the same scales for *blowing* (soloing).

The Ionian, Mixolydian, and Lydian Modes

Time now to make some use of a few other modes. Consider this progression:

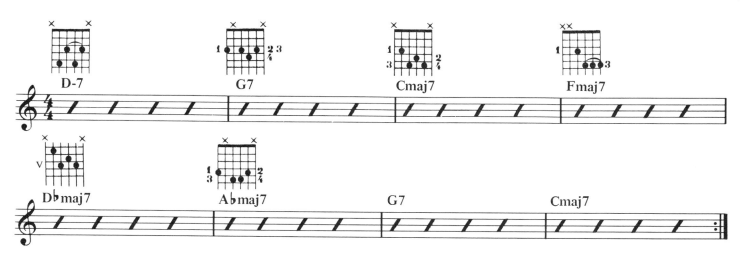

These are the modal scales that you would use for each chord.

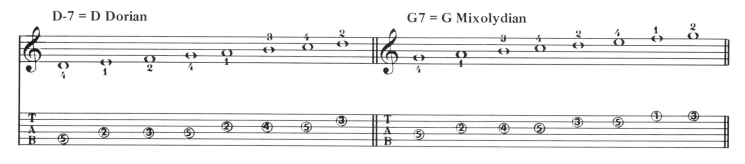

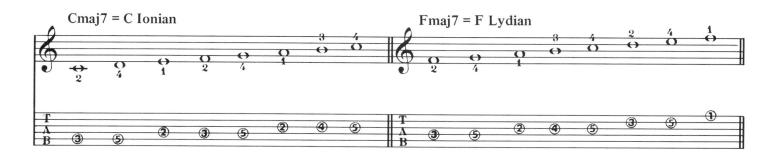

And here is the example complete with melody added.

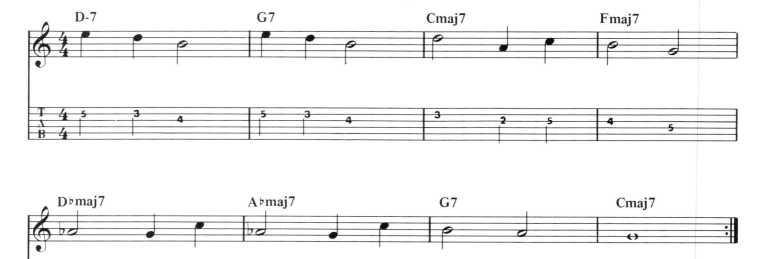

As you begin to catch on to the modal-scale concept you have probably noticed that although the modal scale for each chord is different, it is very often the case that a sequence of several of them will be derived from the same major scale. For instance; in the example above, the first four scales—D Dorian, G Mixolydian, C Ionian, and F Lydian—are all derived from C major. It is important not to get caught in the trap of thinking in C throughout these changes. When you use these scales to improvise, be sure that you observe the shifting tonal centers even though the fingering patterns of some of the scales are identical to others.

Before we examine *when* to use each type of modal scale, let's go over this method which should make it clear *how* to find each scale in any key.

How to Find a Modal Scale

1) You want to play in F Lydian.

2) First ask yourself, "Which major-scale degree corresponds with the Lydian mode?" Ionian is I, Dorian is II, Phrygian is III, and Lydian is IV.

3) Knowing that the Lydian mode is built on the fourth degree of some major scale, you must now ask yourself, "In which major scale is F the fourth degree?" Counting down four degrees from F (F E D C) we arrive at the note C. Therefore, F is the fourth degree of the C major scale: F Lydian scale = C major scale from F to F.

Here is another example:

1) You want to play in B Dorian.

2) Ask yourself, "Which major-scale degree corresponds with the Dorian mode?" Ionian is I, Dorian is II.

3) Now ask yourself, "In which major scale is B the second degree?" Counting down two degrees from B (B A) we arrive at the note A. Therefore, B is the second degree of the A major scale: B Dorian scale = A major scale from B to B.

Here is one more example:

1) You want to play in C Aeolian.

2) Ask yourself, "Which major-scale degree corresponds with the Aeolian mode?" Ionian is I, Dorian is II, Phrygian is III, Lydian is IV, Mixolydian is V, Aeolian is VI.

3) "In which major scale is C the sixth degree?" Counting down six degrees from C (C B A G F E) we arrive at the note E. However, looking at the E major scale, we see that the note C is sharped. So an E major scale will give us a C-sharp Aeolian scale. To play a C-natural Aeolian scale you must use an E-flat major scale from C to C. (You can see how important it is to have a working knowledge of major scales. You will get some help in the chapter, "How to Practice Scales.")

Summary

I am sure that you still have questions about how to use the modal scales you have been playing. The following chart will answer some of them. (The rest will be answered—I hope—by the time you finish this book.) The chart is a summary of which scales go with which chords. These are the basic relationships between the most common chords in any given major key and the modes that they imply. There are no fingerings given with the scales because it is easy to derive a practical way to play any one of them by using any of these three C-major scale patterns.

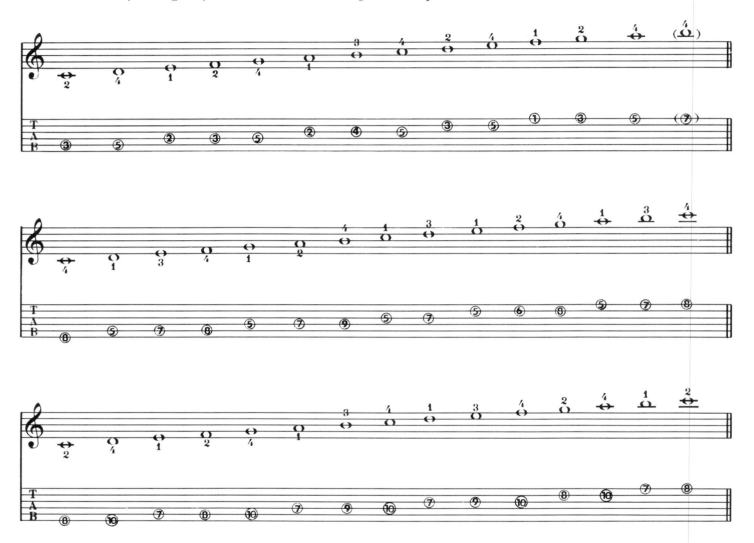

Each one of the modal-scale patterns that you have used to play the examples in this chapter came from one of these three major-scale patterns. Go back and see if you can identify where each modal pattern came from.

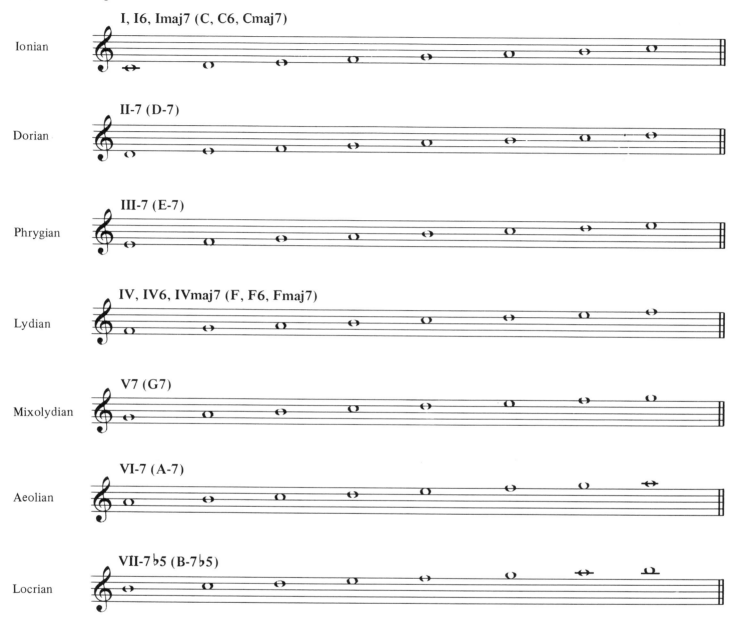

Ionian — I, I6, Imaj7 (C, C6, Cmaj7)

Dorian — II-7 (D-7)

Phrygian — III-7 (E-7)

Lydian — IV, IV6, IVmaj7 (F, F6, Fmaj7)

Mixolydian — V7 (G7)

Aeolian — VI-7 (A-7)

Locrian — VII-7♭5 (B-7♭5)

Harmonizing the Major Scale

In the last chapter you got some practice in major-scale patterns. In this chapter we are going to look at major scales in a different light. This way of looking at scales will help to make clear a lot of things about chord progressions and harmony in general. This will in turn help you with your *comping* (rhythm playing).

Diatonic Seventh Chords

Each note within a scale may be harmonized to create a four-note chord made up of notes only from that scale. I guess that that is an earful but it is really not too difficult to understand. The major scale contains seven different notes and, therefore, we may derive from it seven different chords. (Out of these seven, we have already seen four of them on a pretty regular basis.)

In the first chapter we learned to refer to each scale degree with a Roman numeral.

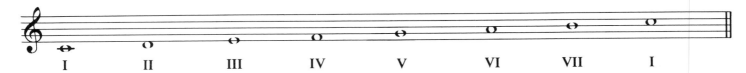

Using only the notes from the scale, we can harmonize each scale degree by adding thirds above it to create these chords.

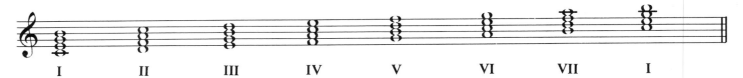

Each of these chords contains only notes from the C major scale. Because of this they are said to be *diatonic* to the key of C. This sequence of chords is often known as the *diatonic seventh* chords of a particular key.

Up to this point we have discussed four different types of diatonic chords: I(maj7), II−7, IV(maj7), and V7. Here they are in the key of C:

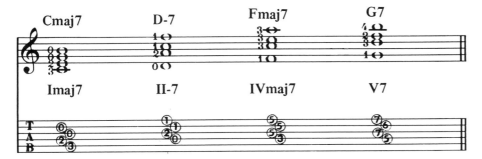

You know from the first chapter that D−7 and F(maj7) are very similar because the F note is an active tone. So we can group these four diatonic seventh chords in this way:

Inactive	Active	"More" Active
Imaj7	II−7 and IVmaj7	V7

Now let's look at the remaining three scale degrees and the chords that they produce. First of all, the three remaining chords (III, VI, and VII) are all minor. The III and VI are both Minor Seventh chords. Let's look at how these chords are constructed.

The III−7 and VI−7 Chords

In the key of C, the III−7 chord is E−7 and is spelled E G B D. The VI−7 is A−7 and is spelled A C E G. Notice the overall abundance of inactive tones; no F or B note in either chord, only a mildly active D note in the E−7. These chords are therefore inactive minor chords when they are used as part of a diatonic chord progression. In other words, if the chord progression uses I, II−, IV, and V chords the III−7 and VI−7 may be substituted for the I chord in order to create an inactive, or "tonic-like," sound. Imaj7 = III−7 = VI−7 because of their inactive tones.

To illustrate just how well this works, let's revive one of our simple tunes from the first chapter.

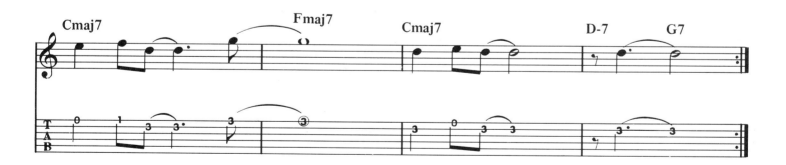

By selectively replacing some of the C Major Seventh chords with E−7 and A−7 chords—plus, don't forget that D−7 may stand in for Fmaj7—we get a variation on the original that begins to sound like something.

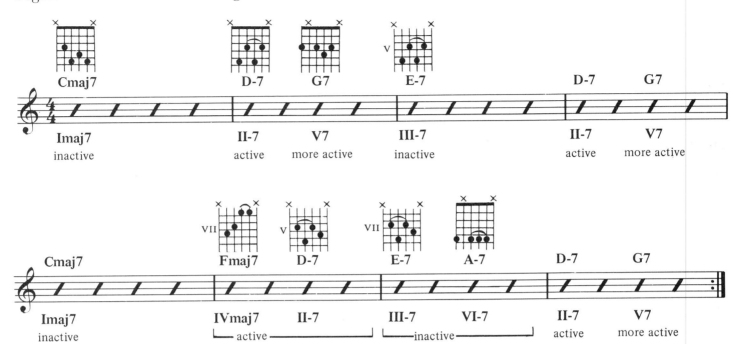

Although the harmonic structure of the chord progression has been changed, the tune sounds pretty much the same as our simpler version of it.

Take some time to play around with this concept applying it to songs or tunes you know. Keep in mind, though, that these are not ironclad rules; sometimes substituting a III−7 or VI−7 for I will sound contrived or, worse, just plain awful. Have fun but let your ear (and your good taste) be your guide.

The VII−7♭5

Let's now look at the remaining diatonic seventh chord, the VII−7♭5 (B D F A in the key of C). (The VII−7♭5 is sometimes called a 'Half-Diminished Seventh' chord and represented by the symbol, ∅7.) Here we have three active tones, B D F, and one inactive tone, A. Clearly this is an active chord considering all of the active tones it contains. In fact, since the active tones of the VII−7♭5 are the same as those of the V7, it often makes a good substitution for the V7. Here are two ways to play B−7♭5; one with the root on the fifth string and the other with the root on the sixth. Try slipping it into some of the progressions above in place of a V7 chord.

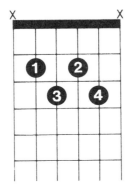 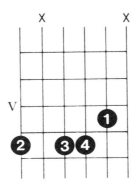

Here is a chart that summarizes the relative amounts of activity and inactivity of all of the diatonic seventh chords:

Inactive	Active	"More" Active
Imaj7	II−7	V7
III−7	IVmaj7	VII−7♭5
VI−7		

Building on I IV V

With this information, we may expand our original understanding of I IV V progressions into an understanding of other progressions; for instance, I II−7 III−7 II−7 V7. This progression is often used as the introduction to a song. It may be repeated over and over until the song actually begins. Progressions used in this way are sometimes referred to as *vamps*. Many times you will see written above an intro like this, "vamp until cue" or "vamp until ready." This means to repeat the progression until the vocalist or soloist is ready to start the song.

Let's try playing this I II III II V vamp in F. As you are vamping, notice how the active G−7 chord bridges the inactive chords Fmaj7 and A−7 on the way up to give a pleasing, scalar type of sound to the progression. On the way down it sets up the V7 chord (II V I).

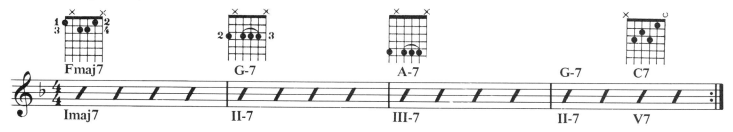

To finish up, let's examine a few progressions that build on our original I IV V blues progression by incorporating diatonic seventh chords. As you practice these examples, try to get used to what the diatonic seventh chords are for each of these three commonly used keys. As an exercise, try playing each one in the key of C by reading the Roman numerals instead of the chord names.

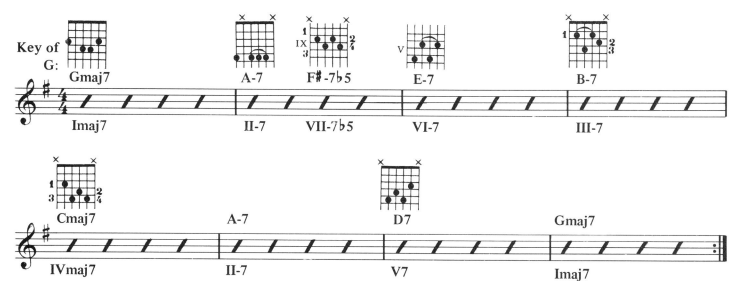

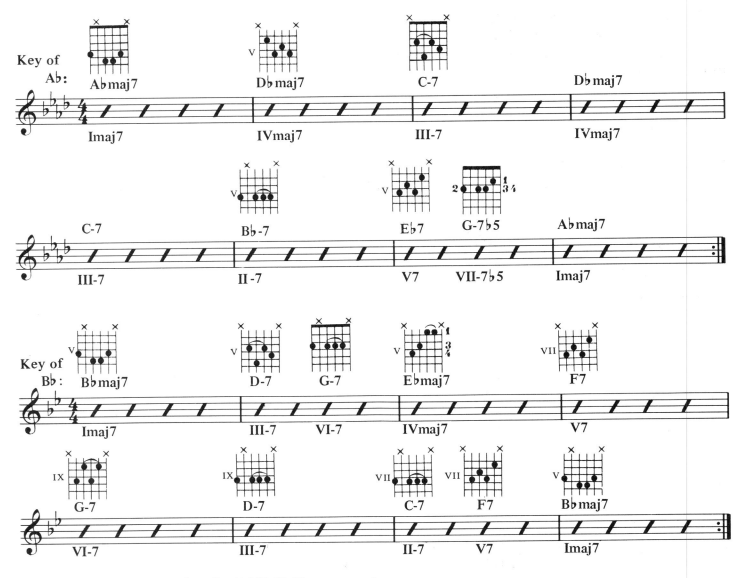

This next is an example of a I VI II V progression; a *very* popular jazz/pop sequence. This sequence, and others like it, is often referred to as *rhythm changes* (named for the Gershwin tune, "I Got Rhythm").

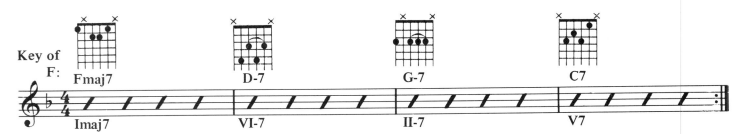

Here are some variations of I VI II V that you are sure to come across. Notice the substitution of III−7 for I in the last two examples. (We will get into the substitutions used for VI and V in the very next chapter.)

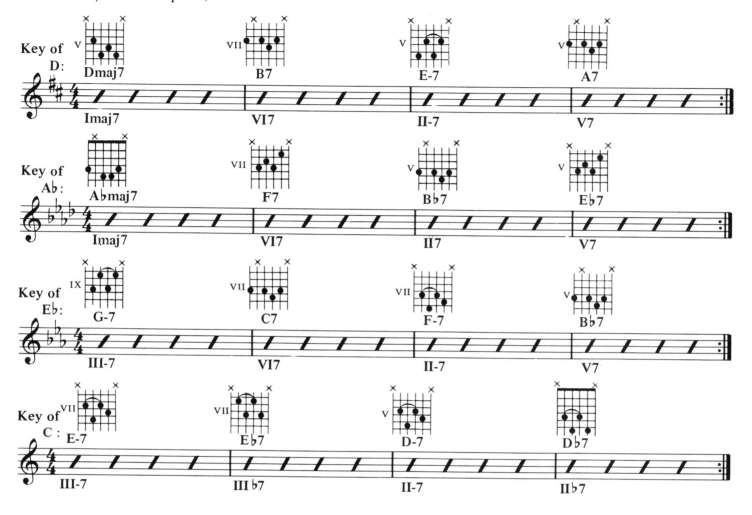

The II-7 V7 Progression

You may well ask, "Why an entire chapter on just two chords?" On the other hand, the fact that the II V sequence crops up so often may have caused you to realize that there is probably something kind of special about it. Let's take a look at what this special quality is.

From what we have learned about inactive and active tones and chords we may say that a diatonic II V I sequence moves from active (II−7) to more active (V7) to inactive (Imaj7). This tension and release produces a kind of climax known as a *resolution* or *cadence*. A typical jazz chord-progression may include several "mini-climaxes" made up of II V sequences causing the tune to wander through as many keys. As an example, play this short progression in the key of C:

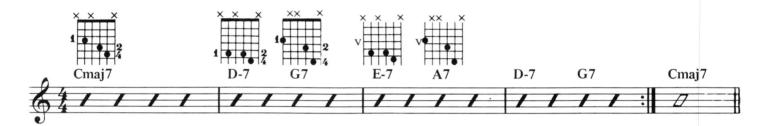

I am sure that all of you immediately realized that D−7 to G7 is II−7 to V7 in C. I hope that you also recognized the following E−7 as the III−7 standing in for the I chord. But what about E−7 to A7 that brings us to the repeat of the C-major II V sequence? These are the II−7 and V7 chords in the key of D. They tell you that the tonality has temporarily shifted from C major to D major. Although this II V sequence in D seems to set you up to go to a D Major chord, the resolution is actually to D−7. This along with the G7 immediately following signals that you are firmly back in the key of C major.

You will want to learn to recognize the II−7 V7 progression whenever it appears. Start analyzing tunes you know and looking through songbooks and fakebooks with an eye to identifying the II−7 V7 sequence. You will find it everywhere! When you recognize a II V, take note if it is diatonic or if it is in a different key. A few perfect examples to get you started:*

"I Got Rhythm" (George Gershwin)

"All the Things You Are" (Jerome Kern)

"Giant Steps" (John Coltrane)

"Tune Up" (Miles Davis)

---

* You will find progressions similar to these and other jazz standards in the section "Solos" in the last chapter.

II V I in Minor

When the II V sequence resolves to a *tonic minor* ('tonic' is another name for 'root' or 'I' so tonic minor = I−), it is common practice to alter the II−7 and V7 to make them II−7♭5 and V7♭9. This variation sets up the minor tonality in a strong and definite manner as you can hear from this II−7♭5 V7♭9 I− in A minor.

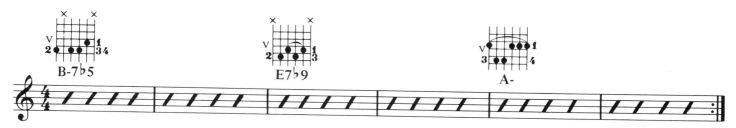

A Common II V Variation

Let's take a look at the properties of the two most active tones of the major scale, the fourth degree and the seventh degree. Together they form what is known as a *tritone*. (The name 'tritone' comes from the fact that this interval consists of three whole-steps.) From the third to the seventh degree of a Dominant Seventh chord is a tritone and it is this dissonant interval that is responsible for the highly active sound of the chord. Here are the tones that make up a G7 chord:

G B D F

I III V VII

From B to F is the tritone interval in this G7. Now let's pull this tritone out of the G7 chord and reverse the functions of the two notes. We can do this because a tritone covers exactly half of an octave: Three whole-steps = six half-steps = one-half of a twelve-tone, chromatic scale ('chromatic' means moving by half steps).

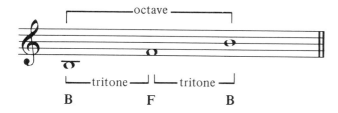

This new tritone, F to B, must belong to a new Dominant Seventh chord. In this new chord F will be the third and B will be the seventh.

? F ? B

I III V VII

Counting down from F (III) to find I, we arrive at the note D.

D E F

I II III

However, a D7 chord has F♯ as its third so D cannot be the root of the new chord we are trying to find. The Dominant Seventh chord that calls F♮ its third is D♭7. Here is the D♭ major scale:

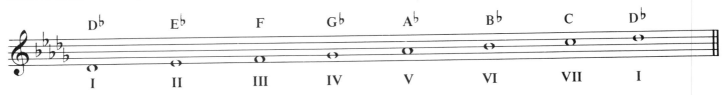

If we pull out the I III V VII from this scale and flat the seventh to make it a Dominant Seventh chord we get D♭ F A♭ C♭. C♭ being the *enharmonic equivalent* of (sounding the same as) B♮, we are sure that our new Dominant Seventh chord is D♭7.

Because these two chords, G7 and D♭7, share the same tritone, B to F and F to B, one can substitute for the other in almost any jazz context.

Here is an example for you to play; you will recognize immediately the familiar sound produced by this common substitution.

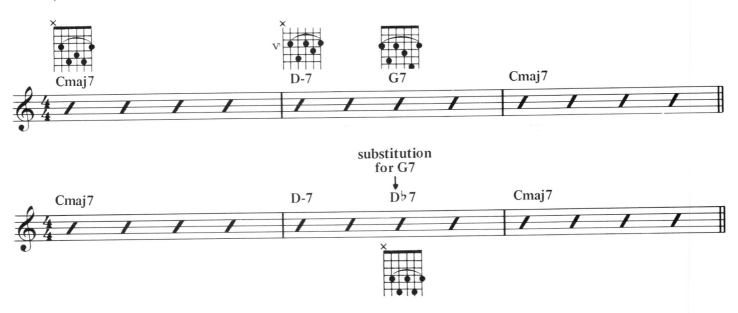

Here is the same progression in G♭.

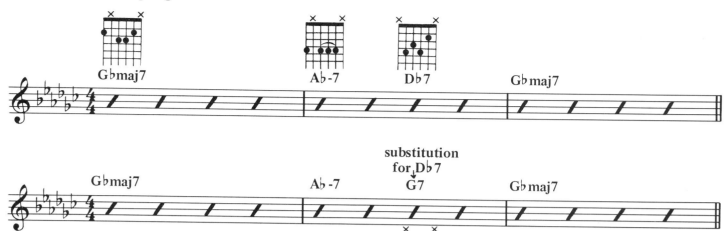

This simple substitution, called *SubV* ("sub-five") produces a characteristic *chromatic resolution* in the bass voice of the chord progression. It is even more obvious in this next example:

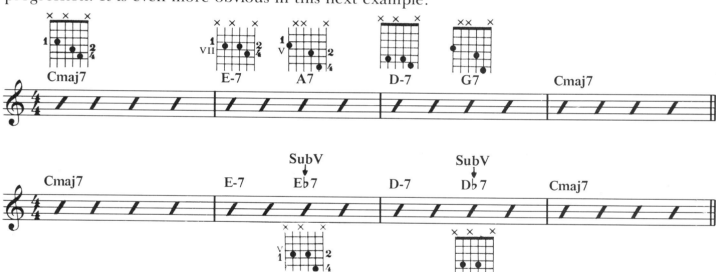

The smooth chromatic motion of E to E♭ to D to D♭ to C sounds really neat.

There are two easy ways to find the SubV without going through the entire process outlined above. One is to remember that its root is a tritone away from the V chord for which you are substituting it. The tritone relationship is an easy pattern to remember on the bass strings of the guitar.

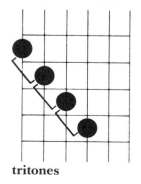

tritones

The other way is to notice that the root of the SubV is always one half-step above the chord to which it resolves.

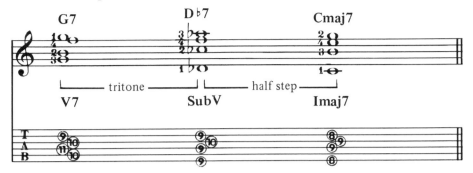

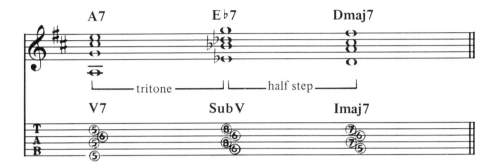

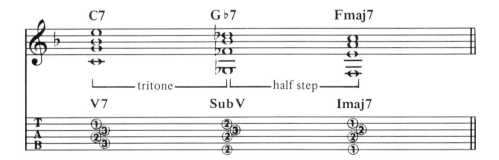

A Further Variation

We can apply the same process we went through with the V7 chord to the II−7 of any II V I progression to produce a *SubII*. In other words, we may substitute a Minor Seventh chord whose root is a tritone away—or one half-step above the root of the chord of resolution—for the II−7.

Where once we had two chords to bring us to I (D−7 to G7), we now have four (D−7 to A♭−7 to G7 to D♭7). This relationship is neatly expressed in this box diagram:

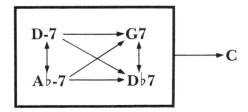

Starting on any of the chords in the box and following the arrows produces an acceptable jazz resolution, or *cadence*. Thus the diagram above translates into the following progressions.

D-7		G7		C
D-7		D♭7		C
D-7		G7	D♭7	C
D-7	A♭-7	D♭7		C
D-7		D♭7	G7	C
D-7	A♭-7	D♭7	G7	C
D-7	A♭-7	G7	D♭7	C
A♭-7		D♭7		C
A♭-7		G7		C
A♭-7		D♭-7	G7	C
A♭-7	D-7	G7		C
A♭-7		G7	D♭7	C
A♭-7	D-7	G7	D♭7	C
A♭-7	D-7	D♭7	G7	C
		G7	D♭7	C
		D♭7	G7	C

Here are two more box diagrams for you to play with. Figure out all of the possibilities contained in each one.

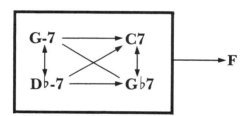

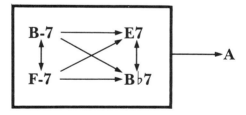

Now, find and write in the SubV chords in the following examples.

We will look into II V progressions some more (including which scales to use for improvising over them) when we get to the chapter, "Playing Through II V Changes and Other Surprises."

How to Practice Scales

Here are four major-scale patterns that you should know. We have already used parts of Types 1, 2, and 4 to find modal patterns in C major.

Type 1: C Major

Type 2: G Major

Type 3: D Major

Type 4: A Major

These four *in-position* scale patterns are all moveable because
they do not use any open strings. Begin practicing each one slowly
until you have learned the pattern. Next try moving each pattern
up the fingerboard keeping track of what key you are in. (Type 1
in second position, as shown above, is a C major scale; so in third
position—up one fret—it becomes C♯ or D♭; in fourth position it
is D; and so on.) Then try playing each pattern starting on the
second, third, fourth, fifth, sixth, and seventh degrees. This way
you can easily create all of the modal scales from any one of these
patterns.

As an example, look what happens when we begin each one of
these scale patterns on E.

Type 1: E Phrygian

Type 2: E Aeolian

Type 3: E Dorian

Type 4: E Mixolydian

Because these four major-scale patterns are each moveable, the modes contained within them are also moveable. Let's start on B♭ (a note that is not found in any of the scales as presented above) and play a Lydian scale using each pattern.

Type 1: B♭ Lydian

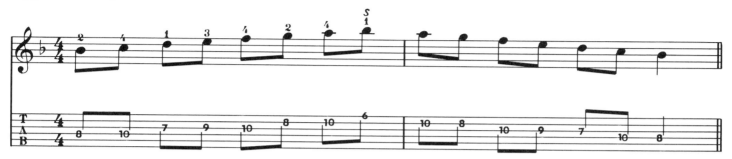

Type 2: B♭ Lydian

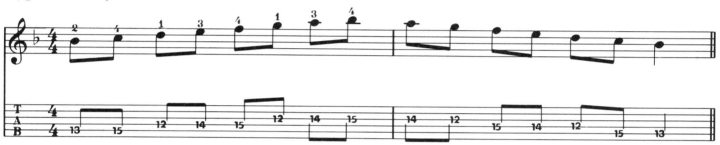

Type 3: B♭ Lydian

Type 4: B♭ Lydian

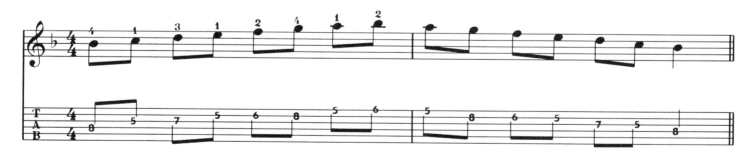

Try this trick with a variety of keys and modes; just follow these steps for each pattern.

    Example: To find G Phrygian using Type 3 major-scale pattern.

1)   Determine on which degree of the major scale the mode begins.

Ionian (major) starts on I

Dorian starts on II

Phrygian starts on III

Lydian starts on IV

Mixolydian starts on V

Aeolian (natural minor) starts on VI

Locrian starts on VII

2) Count up or down to that degree in the scale pattern you are using.

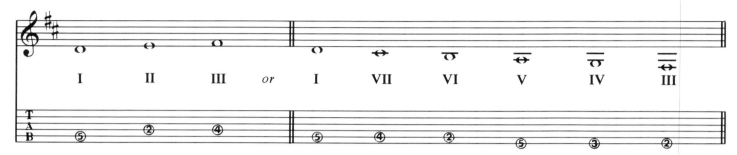

3) Move that note to the tonic of the desired key.

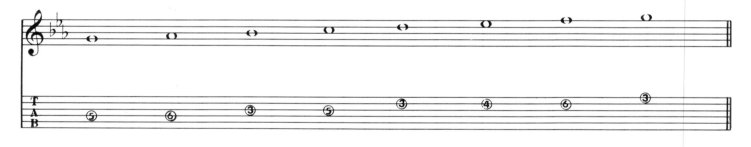

or

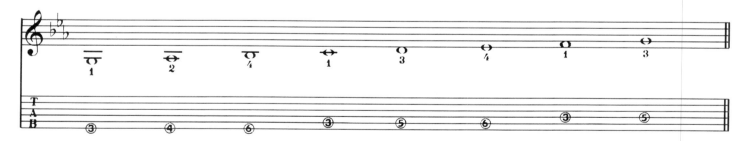

Major-Scale Workouts

After you have begun to get the in-position major-scale patterns under your fingertips, you will need some method for practicing them. The preceding section provides some starting points for developing such an order. Many other ideas and patterns may be found in the method books by Arban, Klose, Hanon, Czerny, and Simandl listed in the Bibliography. Although these are not guitar methods, they are excellent and intriguing sources for scale and chord exercises (plus being good sight-reading practice).

For now, here are some purely guitaristic patterns to use in practicing scales. Use a metronome to keep the beat steady but vary the tempo from time to time. Also try varying dynamics and adding accents so that, although these are purely mechanical patterns, your practicing sounds more musical.

Order for Scale Practice

1) Practice scales moving up and down chromatically.

Type 1: C C♯ D D♯ *etc.*
Type 2: G G♯ A A♯ *etc.*
Type 3: D D♯ E F *etc.*
Type 4: A A♯ B C *etc.*

2) Practice scales going up by whole steps. Use two separate starting points to cover every key.

Type 1: C   D   E   F♯ *etc.*
    C♯ D♯ F   G
Type 2: G   A   B   C♯
    G♯ A♯ C   D
Type 3: D   E   F♯ G♯
    D♯ F   G   A
Type 4: A   B   C♯ D♯
    A♯ C   D   E

3) Practice scales moving around the circle of fifths clockwise.

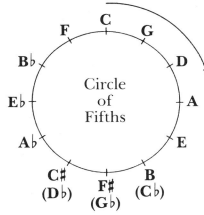

4) Practice scales moving around the circle of fifths counterclockwise (i.e., the circle of fourths).

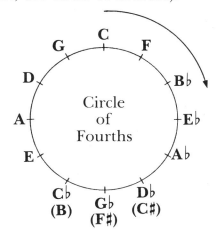

Patterns for Scale Practice

1) Practice scale patterns in diatonic broken seconds, thirds, fourths, fifths, etc.

seconds:

etc.

thirds:

etc.

fourths:

etc.

fifths:

etc.

2) In groups of four notes:

etc.

3) In groups of three notes using triplets (V = down-stroke, ⊓ = upstroke):

etc.

4) In groups of five notes using eighth notes and triplets:

etc.

5) Three scale steps up and a third down:

etc.

6) A third up and three scale steps down:

7) Two more triplet patterns:

Notes on Technique

1) Try to practice your scales with a full, rich tone.

2) Remember to use alternate picking (down-up, down-up).

3) If you aren't already using a medium or stiff (heavy) pick, now is the time to start.

4) Try to break up your practice time. There is no reason to practice for an hour straight if your concentration level begins to drop after twenty or thirty minutes. Take a break and read a book, exercise, or work on your riff diary for a while. Then come back to your scale practice with renewed mental energy.

Up-and-Across Major Scales in C, G, F, and B♭

Ultimately, no matter what pattern you use to practice your scales, you should practice each one starting on the lowest note on your instrument that is part of the scale. For instance, in practicing a C major scale you would start on the open E on the sixth string and end up on the high C on the first string, twentieth fret. For an A♭ major scale you would begin on low F on the sixth string, first fret and continue through to the high D♭ on the first string, twenty-first fret. Of course, deriving the necessary patterns to practice your scales in this way takes some time to work out. Here are four examples and a set of basic rules for good fingering patterns to get you started toward this goal. We call these scale patterns "up-and-across" scales. After you build up some speed practicing them, I think you will see why.

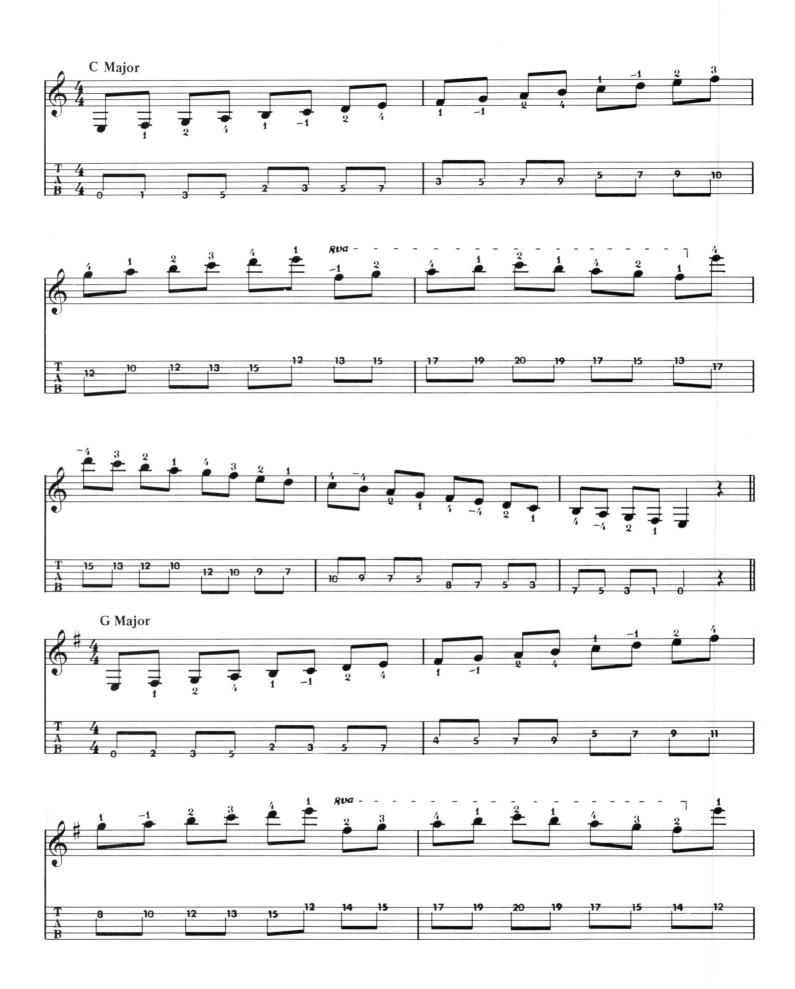

F Major

Bb Major

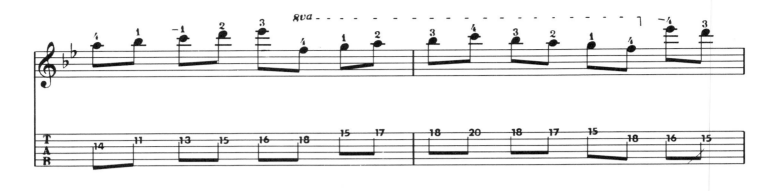

Working Out Fingering Patterns for Up-and-Across Scales

1) Locate the lowest note of the scale that is on the low E string. Sometimes this will be the open E, sometimes the F on the first fret. For instance, the C scale we played above started on the open E; but when you go to work out an E♭ scale, you will want to start on F (the second degree).

2) Starting from either the low E or F play as many notes in the scale as you can in first position on the low E string. You will use one of these three fingering patterns:

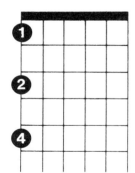
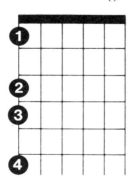
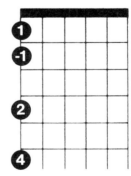

3) Moving over to the fifth string, find the next note in the scale with your first finger.

4) After playing this note move your first finger along the fifth string one or two frets until you come to the next note in the scale. You are now in your next position: Use one of the fingering patterns above to play the next three or four notes in the scale.

5) Repeat steps 3 and 4 on the fourth, third, second, and first strings.

In general, the fingering patterns become fairly automatic as long as you keep in mind that you are always sliding *up* into position each time you move *across* one string. Coming down you apply the opposite rule: Always locate the next note in the scale with your fourth finger as you move *across* to the next lower string and then slide *down* to establish your next position.

Note that the above rules help you to establish the *general* fingering pattern for an up-and-across scale. As you play them you will probably find ways to "break the rules" and smooth out the rough spots. (Keep this in mind as you practice the up-and-across scales that are written out in this book: How do the indicated fingerings break the rules? Why? Can you come up with a better variation?)

For more examples of up-and-across scale patterns, including some scales other than major, see the last chapter.

Playing Through II V Changes and Other Surprises

We have already talked about the ubiquitous II V I progression. We also touched on what happens when the V7 resolves to a I−7 instead of a Imaj7: The I−7 becomes the II−7 of a new II V progression:

II−7   V7   I−7   II−7   V7   I−7
              | | *etc.*
       II−7   V7   I−7

Here is how a sequence of II Vs like this would sound:

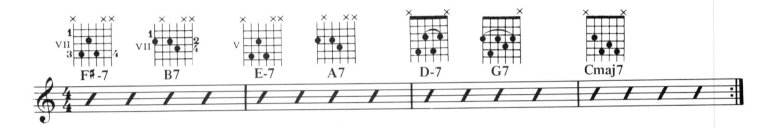

Notice how each II V defines a new key. These temporary 'modulations' (key changes) are strongly felt due to the action of the active tones contained in each II V. A good place to start improvising over this kind of chord progression, is to use the Dorian scale of each II and the Mixolydian scale of each V. Below are some sample solos that will help give you an idea of how you might approach these types of progressions using Dorian and Mixolydian modes.*

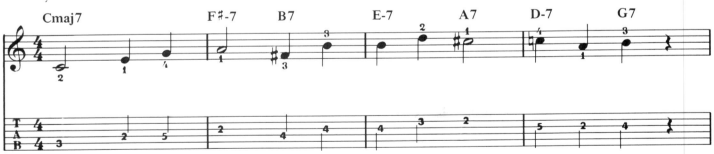

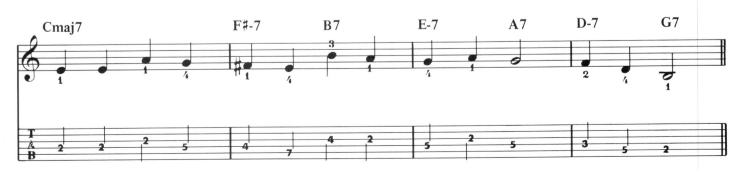

*If some of the major-scale patterns used to derive the modal scales in this and subsequent examples are unfamiliar to you, refer to the section "Scale Patterns" in the last chapter for in-position major scales, types 5, 6, and 7.

50

Now here is a bonus: This progression is a little more complex than the ones above plus it calls for an additional modal scale (besides Ionian, Dorian, and Mixolydian). The reason for using D♭ Lydian in the fifth measure is explained in a few pages but we thought that you might like to try it out now. Here are diagrams for each of the modal scales indicating from which type and position major scale they were derived.

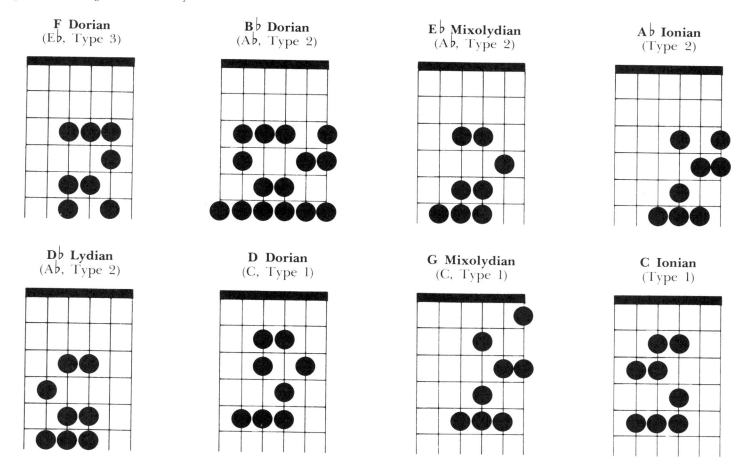

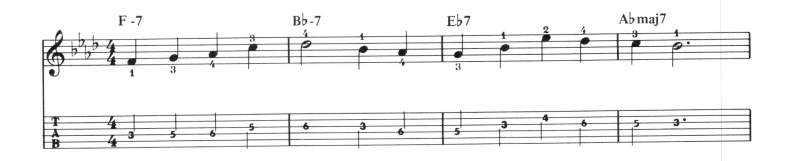

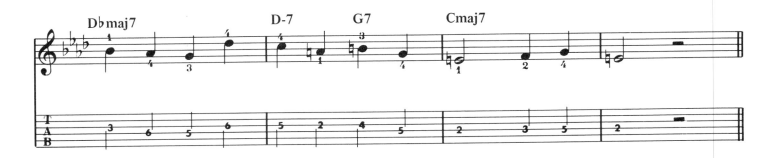

II V I in Minor

Remember the II−7♭5 V7♭9 I−? Sort of like an old friend, right? Let's get into playing some lead over these rather hip sounding changes.

First of all, the general rule for all Minor Seventh Flat Five chords is to use the Locrian mode (major-scale pattern starting on the seventh degree). For example, against a B−7♭5 you would use a C major scale from B to B.

Try these melodies against the II−7♭5 chord. Then try creating your own lines with the Locrian scale.

Now we need a scale for the V7♭9. For this chord we need the *harmonic minor* scale of the tonic minor (I chord). The harmonic minor scale is the same as the Aeolian mode with the seventh degree sharped.

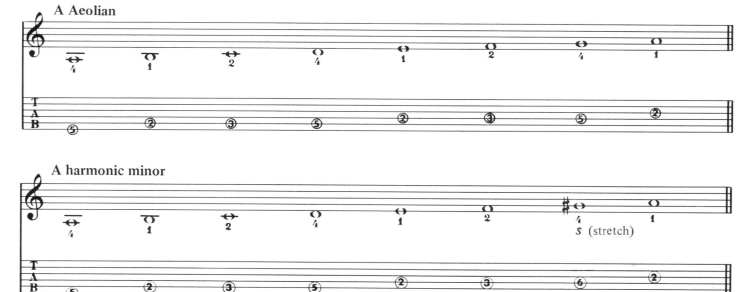

If we compare the A harmonic minor scale to our E7♭9 chord you will see why this is the scale of choice:

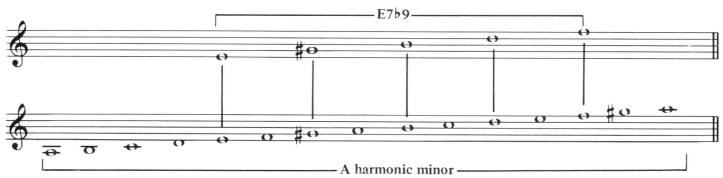

In fact, since the Locrian scale of the II is so similar to the harmonic minor of the I, it is often easier to use the harmonic minor for both the II−7♭5 and the V7♭9. Here are two solos to practice. The first uses the Locrian scale for the II chord and the harmonic minor for the V. The second one features harmonic minor through both II and V. Due to the minor tonality set up by the II−7♭5 to V7♭9 change, you should continue to use the A harmonic minor scale for improvising over the A− chord.

This is beginning to get kind of technical sounding but I hope that you are playing some good lines and are enjoying the new sounds coming from your guitar. If you are having a lot of trouble with this (or any other) section, try to understand as much as you can, practice the scale patterns and chord progressions in the positions shown, learn the practice solos, and move on to the next section. We are starting to cover a lot of ground very quickly but I expect you to really work on this material. Explore each idea as far as you can on your own and you will develop your own personal understanding of it. To this end, don't forget to make note in your "Riff Diary" of any outstanding ideas you may come up with.

Nondiatonic Major Seventh Chords

When we talked about diatonic seventh chords, we said that chords within the key conform to the following arrangement:

Imaj7   II−7   III−7   IVmaj7   V7   VI−7   VII−7♭5

Well, life just isn't quite that simple. In the real world you are liable to see IImaj7s, IV−6s, III7s, and more. Right now we are going to talk about what happens when Major Seventh chords other than I and IV show up. Here is a sample:

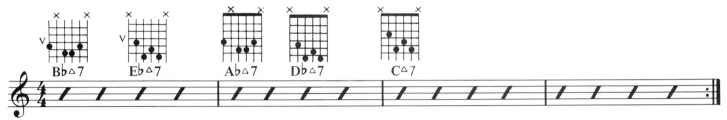

This type of progression makes a good vamp or *turnaround* (a series of chords tacked onto the end of a tune that "turns you around" to the beginning) in C even though it does not contain any diatonic seventh chords except Cmaj7.

The way to treat nondiatonic Major Seventh chords when improvising is as if they were IVmaj7 chords; that is, use the Lydian mode (major-scale pattern starting on the fourth degree). Here is an extended version of our vamp or turnaround plus two more short progressions with the modal scales identified for you:

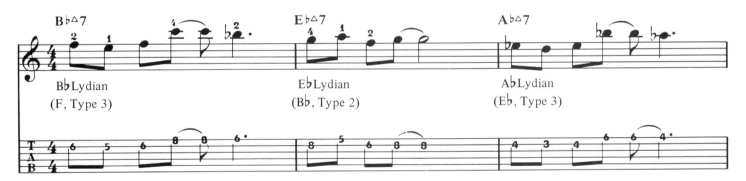

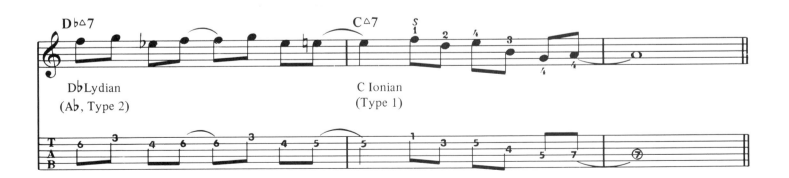

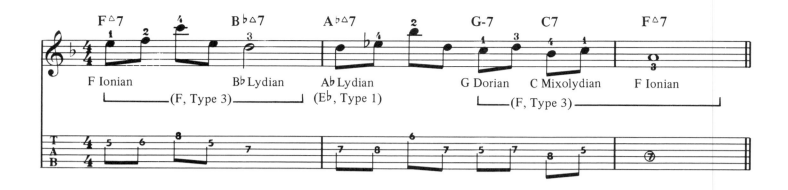

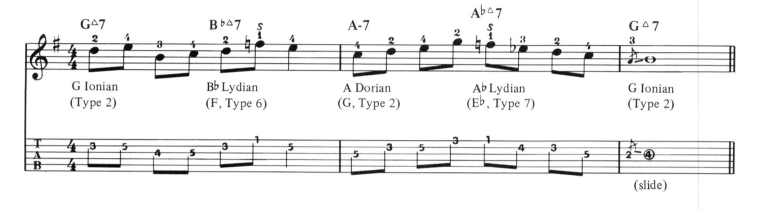

Nondiatonic Dominant Seventh Chords

Dominant Seventh chords from outside the key may also crop up to add color and variety to standard jazz progressions. If they are unaltered (no ♭5s or ♯9s or anything like that), they call for a *Lydian ♭7* scale. As you may well guess, the Lydian ♭7 scale is a variation on the normal Lydian-mode scale in which the seventh is flatted to agree with the flatted seventh of the Dominant Seventh chord.

Another way to think of the Lydian ♭7 scale is as the Lydian mode of the *jazz melodic minor* scale. The jazz melodic minor scale is simply a major scale with a flatted third:

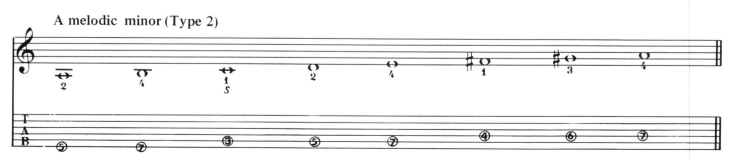

If we derive a Lydian-mode scale from this melodic-minor scale—that is, start on the fourth degree—the resulting scale is a Lydian ♭7.

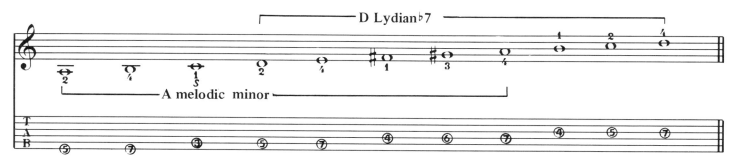

Other ways to arrive at the Lydian ♭7 scale would be sharping the fourth degree of a Mixolydian scale, or sharping the fourth degree *and* flatting the seventh degree of a major scale. (As you can see, the more knowledge you have the more routes you have to arrive at the same destination. This is one of the truly wonderful aspects of the cyclical nature of music.)

Here are a few Lydian ♭7 riffs over a C7 chord. The first three come from the G jazz melodic minor scale that is like G major, Type 2 (also similar to C, Type 1):

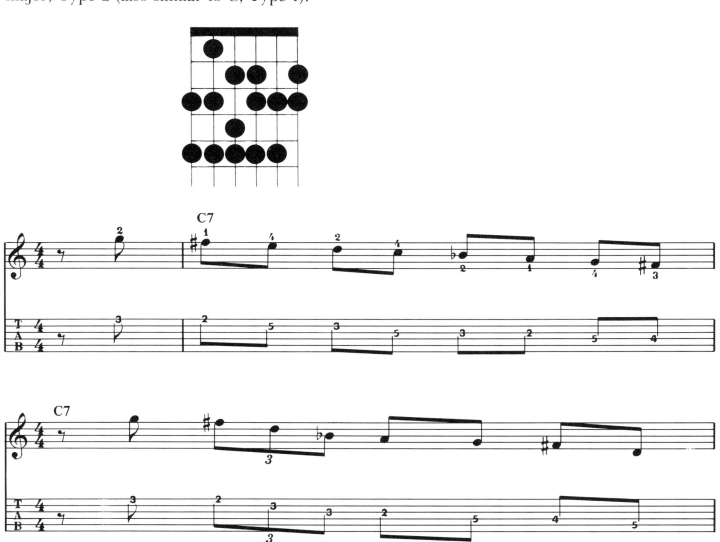

The last two feature the G melodic minor scale that is like G major, Type 4 (also similar to C, Type 2):

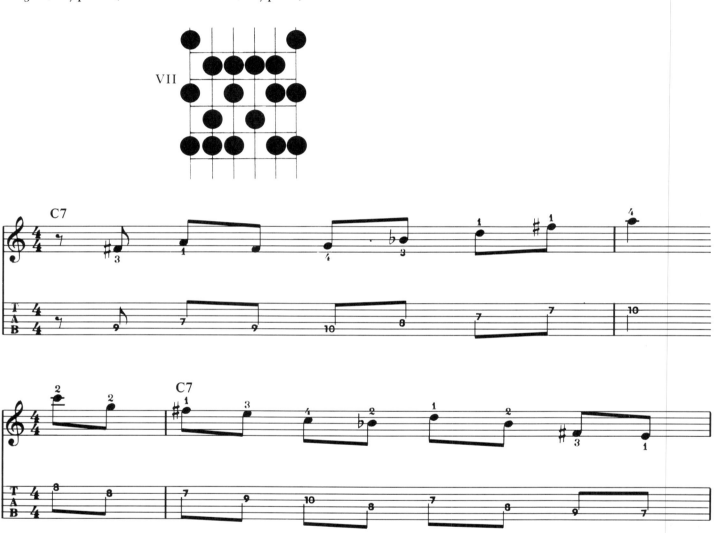

And here are two typical progressions containing a couple of SubV chords that call for Lydian ♭7 scales:

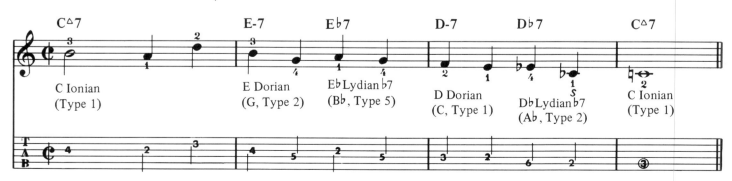

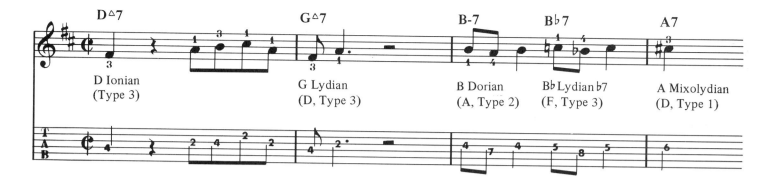

The Other Minor Chords

For improvising over any isolated minor chords that you come across in an otherwise major chord progression the easiest and most natural scale to use is the Dorian mode, same as you would if the minor chord were part of a II V sequence. If the progression is minor, however, you will need to know a bit more about the types of *tonic minor* chords you are liable to come up against.

Tonic Minor Chords

The two basic tonic-minor sounds are the Minor Sixth (−6) chord and Minor(Major Seventh) [−(maj7)] chord. Here is how they sound in G minor:

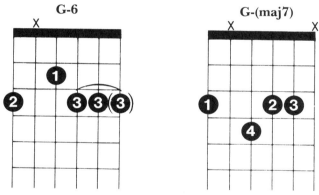

The Minor Sixth chord is simply a minor triad (the same as the one that you would find in a Minor Seventh Chord) with a sixth added. In other words, I III V VI of a jazz melodic minor scale or I ♭III V VI of a major scale.

Minor(Major Seventh) chords are just like Minor Seventh chords with raised sevenths. This is because they are derived from the harmonic minor scale.

Minor Sixth chords call for the jazz melodic minor scale when they are used as tonic minors:

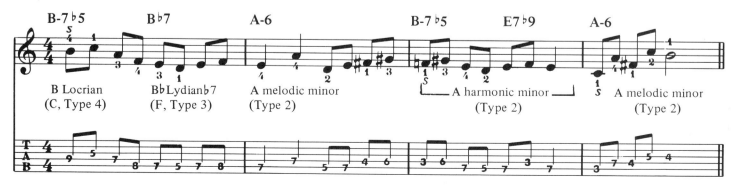

Minor(Major Seventh) chords generally sound best complemented by a harmonic minor scale:

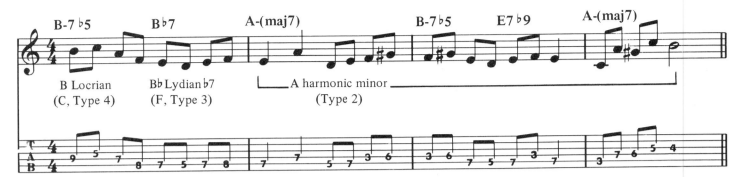

In fact, within the harmonic minor scale lies the origin of the II−7♭5 V7♭9 progression. If we use the harmonic minor scale to derive diatonic II−7 and V9 chords, we find that they both contain the sixth degree of the scale. This note, A♭ in the key of C minor, becomes the flatted fifth of our II−7 chord (D−7♭5) and the flatted ninth of our V9 chord (G7♭9).

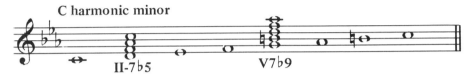

This is why the harmonic minor scale of the tonic minor chord is the one to use for playing through these changes. If you think about it for a moment you will see that it is a direct parallel to using the Dorian and Mixolydian modes when the II V is major.

If you have been keeping up with this cascade of information, take a few moments to catch your breath and maybe give yourself a short round of applause. You may also want to skip ahead now to the last chapter and try learning a few of the standard progressions you will find in the section "Solos." Armed with the "rules" governing which scales to use against each type of chord, try accepting the challenge of soloing over a chorus or two.

Advanced Soloing:

The Diminished Scale, the Whole-Tone Scale, and the Altered Scale

Some New Sounds

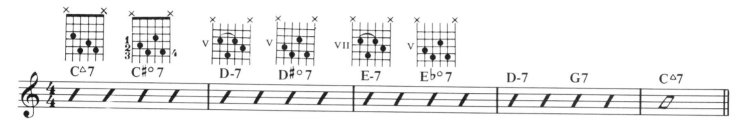

One of the most interesting sounds available to a jazz musician is created by the *Diminished Seventh* chord and its accompanying scale. Let's first take a look at a C Diminished 7 chord (C°7).

The chord is made up of successive minor thirds making it different from the types of chords that we have looked at so far. The Diminished Seventh chord has a "keyless" sound that makes it difficult for the listener to anticipate the next chord. Because of this vague tonality, a Diminished Seventh chord may resolve to almost any other chord. In fact, due to its distinctive symmetry, any of the four notes it contains may be considered the root. So, C°7 is identical with Eb°7 (D#°7), Gb°7 (F#°7), and Bbb°7 (A°7). Play this short sequence and you will see and hear how this is so.

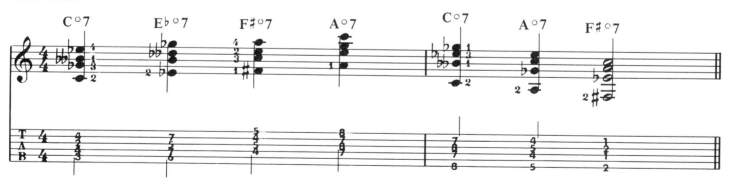

All of the chords in the above progression could be considered to be C°7s; or they could all be Eb°7s or F#°7s, and so on. The way that the Diminished Seventh chord is made up of superimposed minor thirds causes it to "repeat" every three frets (three half-steps = minor third).

Here are three more progressions to give you a chance to familiarize yourself with Diminished Seventh chords.

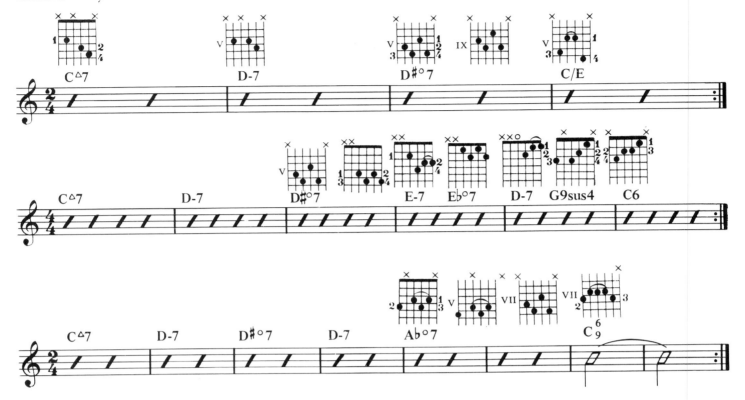

The first two examples above use Diminished Seventh chords as *passing* or *bridge chords*. Passing chords produce intriguing chromatic resolutions in the bass line and in the inner voices. In the third example the Ab°7 functions a bit differently. If you look at the last four measures you will see a II−7 (D−7) moving to a chord with a highly active sound (Ab°7) resolving to a I (C $\frac{6}{9}$). Could this mystery chord actually be some type of V in disguise? The answer, of course, is yes: The Ab°7 is substituting for the V7, G7. The reason that this substitution works is the same reason that the SubV substitution works: The Ab°7 contains the tritone that defines the G7 chord, B to F. Let's spell the Ab°7 as a G♯°7 to compare it to the G7.

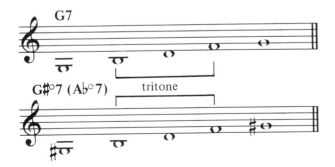

The only difference is the G♯ (Ab) note in the G♯°7. This note, when added to the G7 chord, becomes a *tension* and makes the G7 into a G7b9 chord. (You have already played Dominant Seventh Flat Nine chords when we went over II V in minor.)

This substitution is extremely handy and easy to remember: For any Dominant Seventh chord just play the Diminished Seventh chord whose root is one half-step higher to produce a Dominant Seventh Flat Nine without the root. (The strong sound of the tritone [B and F] and the flat nine [A♭] resolving chromatically to the tones of the I chord make the root of the V7♭9 unnecessary.)

Here is an example of a typical II V progression presented first straight and then with V7♭9 substitutions.

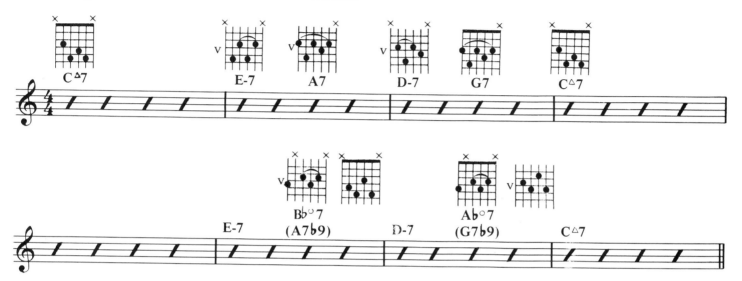

And here is a bonus: Since you know that any note in a Diminished Seventh chord may be considered its root, each Diminished Seventh chord may stand in for any one of four Dominant Seventh chords. Looking back to the structure of the G♯°7 above and applying the half-step-higher rule we can say that the G♯°7 (or A♭°7) equals G7♭9, B♭7♭9, D♭7♭9, and E7♭9. Add to this the fact that °7 chords repeat every three frets and you have a powerful way to get around the neck on a V7 chord. Try these two progressions in which we use the various forms of the °7 substitution for 7♭9; first ascending,

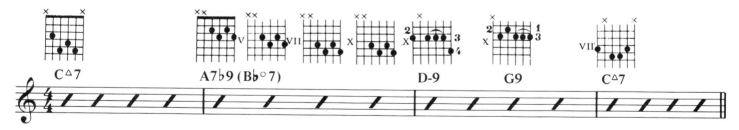

then descending.

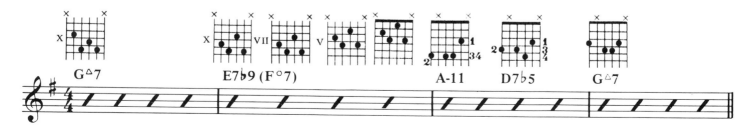

Try going back over some of the progressions in the chapter
"The II−7 V7 Progression" that use Dominant Seventh Flat
Nine chords using this Diminished Seventh substitution. Then
try it out as a substitution for any V7 chord in other progressions you know.

Diminished Scales

The tonal ambiguity of the Diminished Seventh chord carries
over into the *diminished scale*—just listen:

As you can see, the diminished scale is made up of alternating
whole steps and half steps. (It is important to remember to start
the scale with a whole step; otherwise a diminished scale one
half-step away from the one you want will result.)

There are only three distinct diminished scales.

The reason for this should become clear as you start to use them. For now, let's try a practical example of a progression employing a typical II V I sequence with the addition of a Diminished Seventh chord. As you get the hang of it, try making up your own lines for the example using the same scales.

This next example uses a new pattern for the diminished scale. We will call this one Type 2 and the pattern presented above Type 1.

Diminished scale pattern

The example above uses the Diminished Seventh as a passing chord. This one uses a Diminished Seventh chord—and its diminished scale—as a 7♭9 substitution for the Dominant Seventh

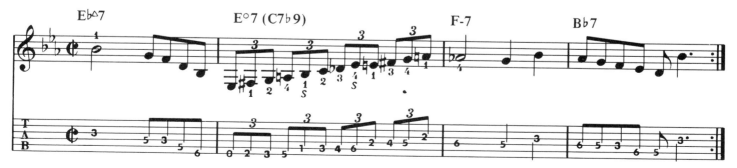

Finally, here is another short progression using a °7 as a bridge chord. Notice that we use the diminished scale (Type 1 again) a bit more musically here, rather than strictly stepwise.

The Whys and Wherefores of Diminished Chords and Scales

Now that you have been playing diminished chords and scales for a little while you have probably begun to catch on to some of their unusual properties. Let's review and examine some of these properties a bit more closely.

Because each of the four notes in a Diminished Seventh chord may function as its root (giving the chord four possible names), there are only three distinct Diminished Seventh chords (and hence only three distinct diminished scales). This is because we have only twelve different notes in our chromatic scale. Think about this as you try playing this example:

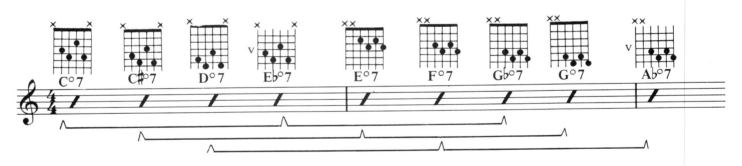

You can hear that the E♭°7 and G♭°7 are extensions of the C°7, the E°7 and G°7 extensions of the C♯°7, and the F°7 and A♭°7 extensions of the D°7.

Now try the scales:

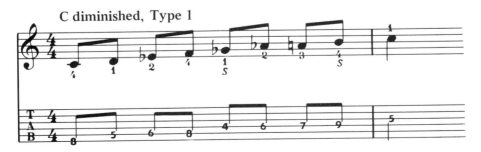

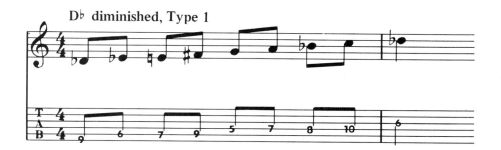

D♭ diminished, Type 1

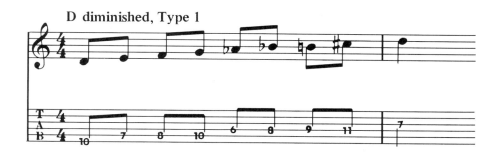

D diminished, Type 1

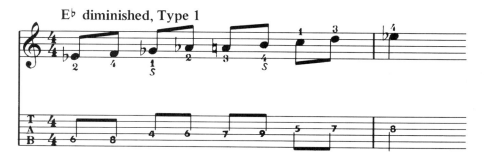

E♭ diminished, Type 1

You can see how the pattern is the same for scales whose roots are a minor third (one and one-half steps) apart.

Here is another way to think of the ways in which the three Diminished Seventh chords and scales relate to one another:

$$C°7 = E♭°7 = G♭°7 = A°7$$

$$C♯°7 = E°7 = G°7 = A♯°7$$

$$D°7 = F°7 = A♭°7 = B°7$$

$$E♭°7 = G♭°7 = A°7 = C°7$$

etc.

Each line above shows the four different names that each Diminished Seventh chord may have. Each set is one half-step higher than the one before. Notice that the last line is a repeat of the first. If you were to continue the sequence starting the next line with E°7, you would get a repeat of the second line.

From the brief examples you have played, you have heard that the diminished scale sounds right for improvising over diminished chords. In case you are wondering how such a strange scale came to be, here is a quick explanation of why the diminished scale and chord go together so well. Look back at one of the C°7 scales above. If you pick out every other note from this scale, they spell out a C°7 chord. Since a C°7 chord is identical to an E♭°7, G♭°7, or an A°7, it makes sense that a C°7 scale is identical to an E♭°7 scale, G♭°7 scale, or an A♭°7 scale. The symmetry is such that any of these four notes may be the root of the scale. Try this with the other two diminished scales.

Well that's enough theoretical musing for a while; let's do a little more playing.

Other Applications of the Diminished Scale

The most interesting application of the diminished scale is the 7♭9 substitution we touched on earlier. Remember the rule: Use a diminished chord, and scale, whose root is one half-step above the root of the Dominant Seventh chord. Play the example below and listen to what the A♭°7 scale does to the simple G7 to C sequence:

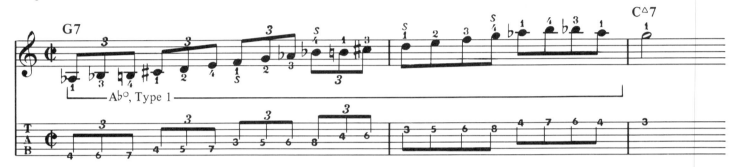

Here are two short II V I progressions featuring diminished scales over Dominant Seventh chords.

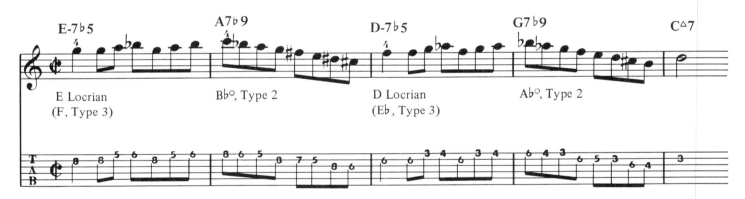

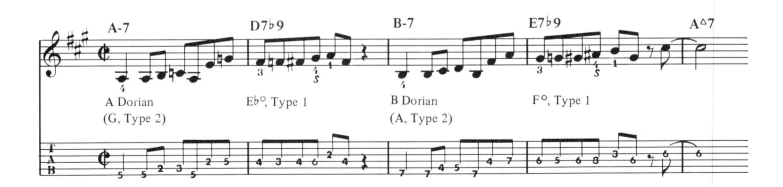

68

Tensions, *or* Those Funny, Little Numbers with Sharps and Flats

If you have ever tried to figure out a song or tune from a fakebook or piece of sheet music, you have probably come across at least a couple of chord names that were a bit of a mystery; they have weird, exotic names like D♭7♭9 or F♯9♭5 or even A♭13$^{♯11}_{♭9}$. If you have a good ear you have probably figured out that for most of the these chords with the "funny, little numbers with sharps and flats" you can get away with playing normal Dominant Seventh chords (like D♭7, F♯7, and A♭7). If you know how a Dominant Seventh chord is constructed, it is easy to see where the additional numbers come from and what they signify.

Let's begin our exploration of *tensions* by taking apart a good old G7 chord:

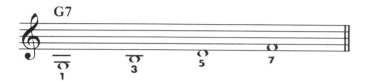

As we all know (or, if we don't, can see by the example above) a Dominant Seventh chord is made up of 1 3 5 7 but the notes come from the major scale whose root is a fifth below (remember, *dominant* = fifth degree of the scale). If we continue this pattern of superimposed thirds, we come next to 9 ♯11* 13. Notice that these are an octave above the 2, 4, and 6, respectively:

When you see a chord name followed by one of these numbers, it implies that the chord contains the numbers below as well. This is very often impractical on guitar since we have only six strings and five fingers. For instance, a complete G13 chord would sound like this (in arpeggio):

---

*Since the natural 11 conflicts with the third of the chord (11 = sus4) it is almost always replaced with the ♯11.

If you wanted to play the complete chord all at once, you would have to leave something out (the chord has seven notes). Here is a tortured position for G13 omitting the fifth:

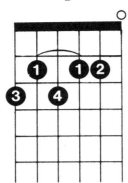

Yecch! So what *do* you play when you see the chord symbol G13? Maybe you already know one or two of these positions. Figure out what is missing from each one, and then check your answers against those given below.

G13   D13   C13

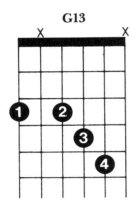 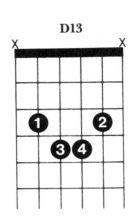 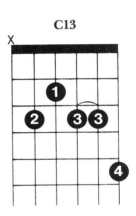

A♭13   B♭13   A13   F13

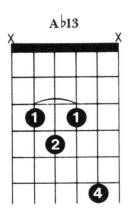 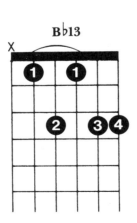 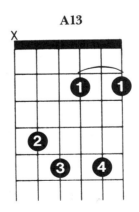 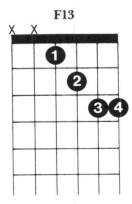

G13: 5, 9, ♯11; **D13:** 5, 9, ♯11; **C13:** 5, ♯11; **A♭13:** 1, 5, ♯11; **B♭13:** 9, ♯11; **A13:** 9, 11; **F13:** 1, 5, ♯11.

Now, what does all this have to do with using the diminished scale to improvise over Dominant Sevenths? And what about the sharps and flats that go with the "funny, little numbers"? Here is the answer to both questions. When we were considering the diminished scale for improvising over Diminished Seventh chords, we found that all of the notes of the chord were contained within the scale. Now let's compare our A♭°7 scale to a G7 chord and see how the two compare:

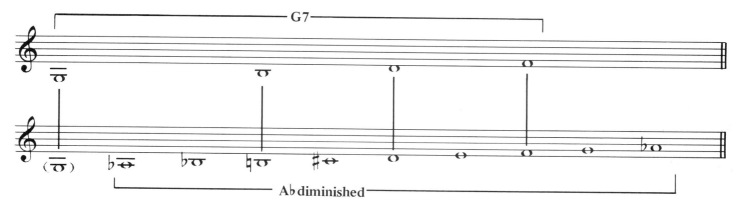

So far, so good; but what about 9 ♯11 13? Glad you asked . . .

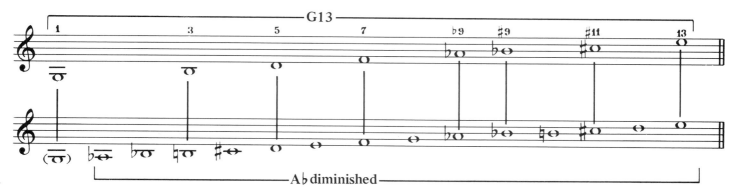

Now we are beginning to get into some weird terrain. Before going any farther, let's take a moment to listen to some of the sounds described by these tensions. First, a chord not derived from the diminished scale (because the scale skips over the natural 9), the Dominant Ninth:

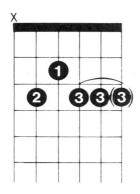

Now the Dominant Flat Nine:

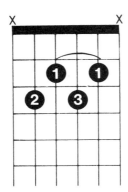

The Dominant Sharp Nine:

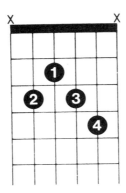

Dominant Sharp Eleven:

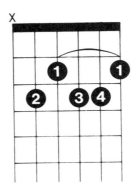

(The Natural 11 is used almost exclusively with minor chords.)

We will be talking more about these upper tensions and using the diminished scale for improvising right after we discuss another symmetrical scale called . . .

The Whole-Tone Scale

The way that this scale is usually used is over an Augmented (or Augmented Seventh) chord. An Augmented chord is a major chord with a sharped fifth and is indicated by the symbol +:

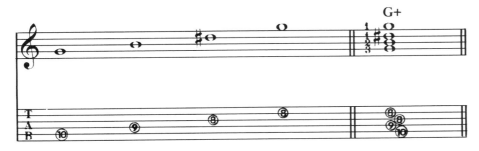

72

"G+7" would indicate the addition of the dominant seventh:

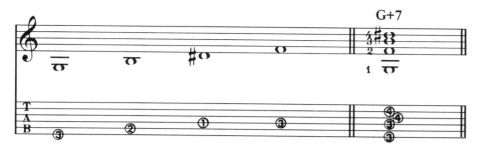

As its name implies, the whole-tone scale is made up of successive whole tones:

Let's compare the G whole-tone scale to the G+7 chord:

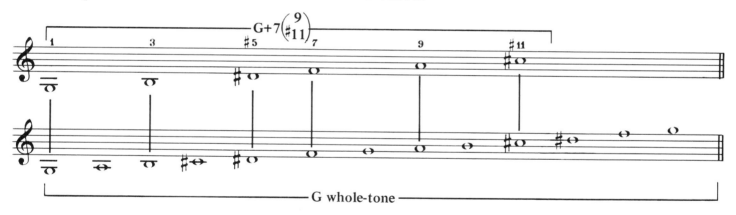

As you can see, the scale contains all of the notes in the chord plus the second (or *ninth*, if you take it up an octave) and the flatted fifth (sharp eleven). This is definitely the scale of choice for any Dominant Seventh (or Ninth) chord with a sharped fifth!

An example of the whole-tone scale in action may be heard in the intro to Stevie Wonder's "You Are the Sunshine of My Life." The ascending melody and harmony is created by whole-tone scales in parallel thirds. (A less musical, but decidedly more peculiar example of the whole-tone scale is the old radio jingle for a nasal spray called Sine-Off.)

There are even fewer distinct whole-tone scales than there are diminished scales: two. If you transpose a whole-tone scale up one whole-step you are right back where you started. In other words, two whole-tone scales one half-step apart contain all twelve tones found in Western music (which includes most jazz).

From this line of reasoning it is a small leap to the realization that any note in a given whole-tone scale may be considered the root of the scale.

Here are a Type-2 pattern and two progressions with sample melodies employing the whole-tone scale concept. Again, once you see how it all fits together, try using the same scales to create your own lines over these changes.

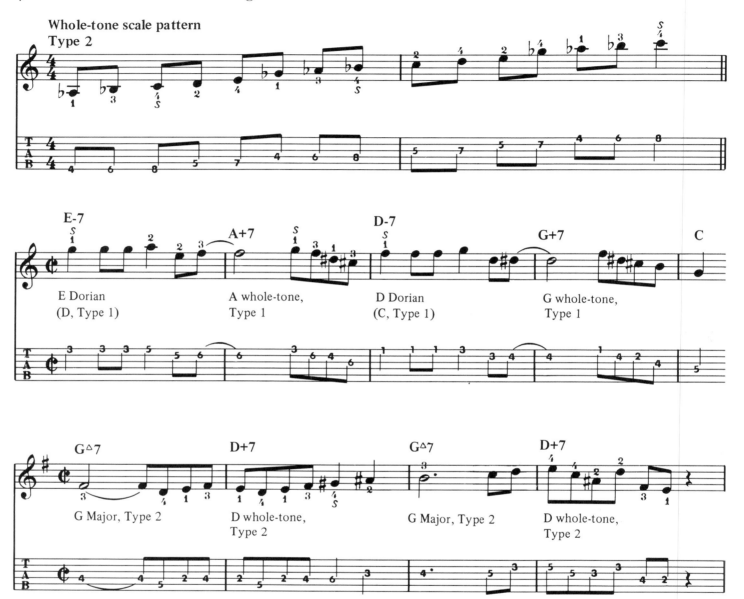

The Altered Scale

When we looked at the tensions contained in the diminished scale, you may have remarked that there were two common ones missing: the natural 9 and the sharp 5. Then we looked at the whole-tone scale against a Dominant Seventh chord and found that it added these two missing tensions. Now comes the *altered scale* in which all tensions live together in resplendent harmony (or at least in amiable dissonance). To explore this hybrid scale, let's stick to our benchmark, G Dominant Seventh (key of C).

First, the A♭ diminished scale (starting on G),

Next, the G whole-tone scale,

Now, combine the first tetrachord (*tetra* = four, *chord* = note; Greek, you know) of the diminished scale and the second tetrachord of the whole-tone scale:

Voilà, the altered scale. If we extend the altered scale to two octaves and apply the (by now) old trick of comparing the altered scale to the G7 chord we can see that the scale contains all of the upper tensions inherent in both the diminished and whole-tone scales.

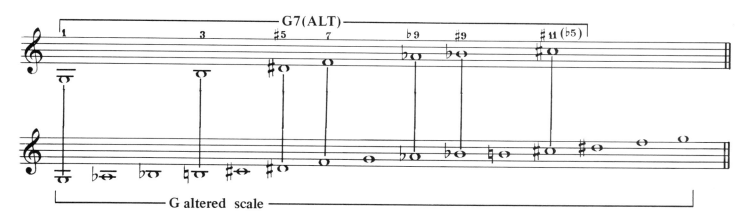

The only chord tones that are not altered are the 1, 3, and 7. Both the 5 and the 9 have been first flatted then sharped. These alterations are indicated when you see a chord symbol like "G7(ALT)." For chord voicings, the rule is to play ♭5 *or* ♯5, and ♭9 *or* ♯9 but never ♭5 *and* ♯5, or ♭9 *and* ♯9. In simpler terms:

G7(ALT) = G7♭5/♭9 or G7♭5/♯9 or G7♯5/♭9 or G7♯5/♯9

Never play a chord like G7♭5/♯5 or G7♭9/♯9 or G7♭9/♯9/♯5 (unless it's a request).

There are a lot of different fingerings for altered scales but here are four in-position patterns that you will find useful.

To finish off, we leave you with some more examples to play through. As before, utilize the indicated scales to make up leads of your own. The sky's the limit . . .

Bonus Chapter: Scales, Solos, and Other Fun Stuff

In this chapter we hope to give you a summary of some of the information that has been presented. This also seemed like the place to present a few techniques and touches that didn't really fit in with any of the other chapters or that look at some of the previously presented ideas in a slightly different light.

Keep in mind that there is no one set way of presenting the theory of jazz improvisation. All you have to do to see the truth in this is to listen to a few of the many players whose styles may be different as night and day but all of whom play jazz. The concepts presented in this book are all solid, tried and true information organized in a way that we hope you have found easy and fun to understand and use. However, if you now have a good command of this information, it would be a good idea to start checking out other jazz method books. This will go a long way toward reinforcing, and hence helping you to apply, your understanding of these ideas.

As you begin to delve into other jazz instruction books (several are recommended in the Bibliography) try to be patient. Remember that up until the last decade or so there were no real methods available to musicians wishing to learn the theory and practice of jazz improvisation. Even now, with many excellent books easily available, it takes most players years of playing and experimenting to develop a true working knowledge of the many musical tools of the jazz improviser. It takes much more playing and practice to use these tools with style.

Chord Scales for Diatonic and Nondiatonic Chords

Scales for Major Chords

I	Ionian (major)
IV	Lydian
II	Lydian
VI	Lydian
VII	Lydian

Scales for Minor Seventh Chords

II−7	Dorian
III−7	Phrygian
IV−7	Dorian
VI−7	Aeolian
VII−7♭5	Locrian
II−7♭5	Locrian

Scales for Dominant Seventh Chords

V7 (to major chord)	Mixolydian or altered
V7 (to minor chord)	harmonic minor a fifth below or altered
II7	Lydian ♭7 (jazz melodic minor a fifth above)
II7	Lydian ♭7
IV7	Lydian ♭7
I7	Lydian ♭7

Scale Patterns
In-Position Patterns

Here are three in-position major-scale patterns that were not introduced in the body of the book (although parts of them were used in a few of the examples).

Type 5: B♭ Major

Type 6: F Major

Type 7: E♭ Major

Up-and-Across Patterns

In the chapter "How to Practice Scales" you were introduced to up-and-across patterns for C, G, F, and B♭ major. Here are the rest of the major scales as well as patterns for the other types of scales that we have been using.

Major Scales

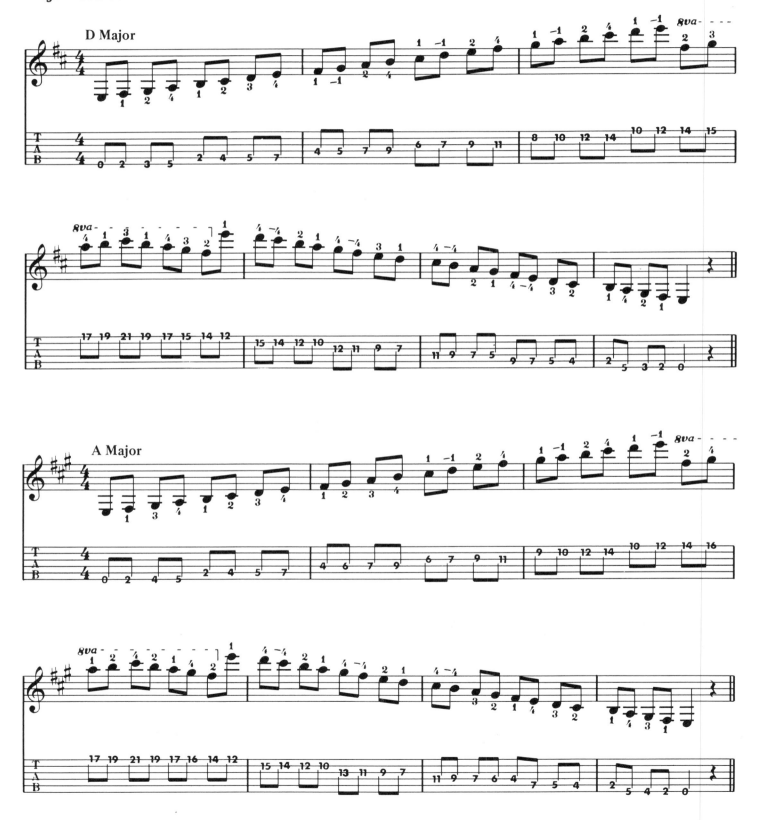

E Major

B Major

E♭ Major

A♭ Major

Harmonic Minor Scales

F Harmonic Minor

Jazz Melodic Minor Scales

C Jazz Melodic Minor

Diminished Scale

Whole-Tone Scale

Altered Scales

Fun with Triads

Here are three chords that you have probably been using since about the second week that you were playing guitar.

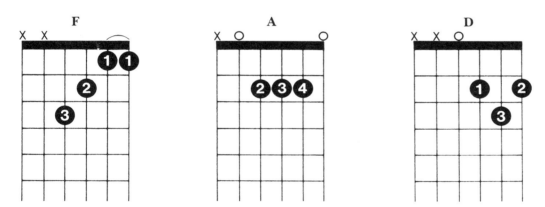

All three are basic, first-position triads—no sixths, sevenths, ninths, etc. You can use these simple positions to produce some pretty powerful tensions simply by playing them above different bass notes. Let's take the F position shown above and put a G in the bass.

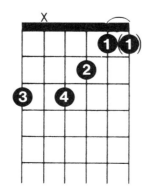

This is quite a different chord from the basic F triad. In fact it is not an F chord at all. By putting the G in the bass we have changed it to some sort of G chord. The notes of the F triad (F A C), which are inactive tones relative to F, are all active tones against the G tonic. By considering them in this light, we can see that what we have created is a G9sus4.

If we think of G9sus4 as a Dominant Seventh in the key of C, we have a form of V7 that is not as active as a straight G7 chord but rather closer to IVmaj7 or II−7.

There are lots of ways to produce unusual chord voicings by placing triads over seemingly unrelated bass notes. These chord forms are often referred to as *slash chords* due to the practice of naming them with a chord symbol like this: F/G ("F over G").

The G9sus4 chord above was produced by superimposing a triad whose root is one whole-step below the bass note. Now let's do the same thing with a triad whose root is one whole-step higher that the bass note; in other words, A/G:

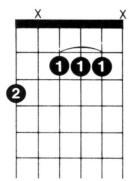

Congratulations. You have just played a G9$^{6}_{\sharp 11}$ chord. (With names like G9sus4 and G9$^{6}_{\sharp 11}$ you can see why some musicians refer to these chords by their slash-chord names.) Now try this II V I progression. By simply playing A−7 to C/D to A/G you are actually playing II−7 to V9sus4 to I9$^{6}_{\sharp 11}$ in G.

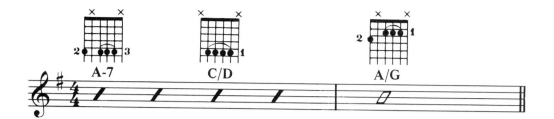

Another slash chord to try is the one produced by the triad whose root is a sixth above the bass note. This results in a Dominant Thirteen Flat Nine. In other words,
A/C = C13♭9 *or* F♯/A = A13♭9:

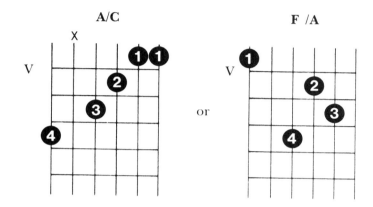

Here is an easy way to get good voicings for ALT. chords. (Remember that an ALT. chord is a Dominant Seventh with an altered fifth and ninth.) Use the triad whose root is a tritone above (or below) the bass note: D♭/G = G7$^{♭5}_{♭9}$,

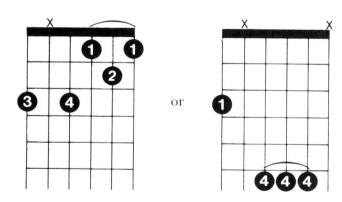

and F♯/C = C7$^{♭5}_{♭9}$.

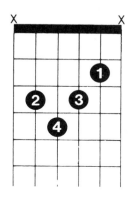

Changing triads over a common bass note can produce intriguing examples of voice leading like the following.

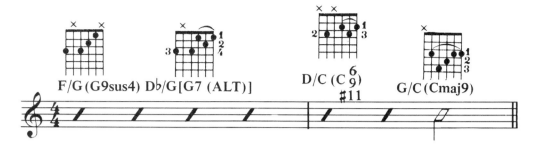

Here is an example using C and D triads over an A to produce minor tonalities.

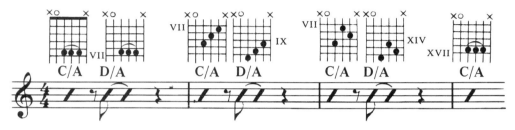

Your Inner Ear: That Part of the Mind That Hears and Creates Music

A jazz musician singing along with his or her instrument while improvising is a perfect example of the inner ear at work. The melodies created by improvising are first heard by the inner ear (mind) and expressed through the voice and/or instrument.

Understanding and using this concept is of vital importance. Singing along with recorded solos is a good way to begin programming your inner ear to hear jazz lines. Playing chords on the guitar or piano and singing the corresponding scale is also a useful thing to do. For example, play a C chord then sing a C major scale. Do this until your voice feels comfortable and then pick and choose notes from the scale to make up melodies. This is how the creative process of improvising begins to take shape. Some of the most famous jazz musicians, including Dizzy and Miles, have used this concept to help unlock their inner ears.

Below are a few more "exercises" for your ear . . .

1) *Try to copy another player's melodic lines.* You can do this by playing along with records or by getting together with other players (not necessarily guitarists) and taking turns mimicking each other.

2) *Hum familiar melodies and try finding them on your instrument.* Any melody will do; "The Star-Spangled Banner," "The Farmer in the Dell"—I'm talkin' *any* melody! Also, sing along with your guitar as you practice scales. Learn to use your voice. It will become the vital link between your ear and your instrument.

3) *Over a stationary chord, sing melodies that are composed of either all active or all inactive tones.*

C (△7)

active tones

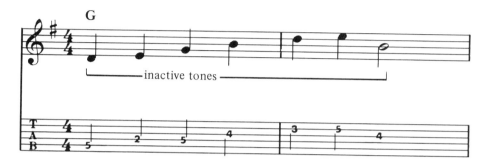

G

inactive tones

Then try mixing active and inactive tones.

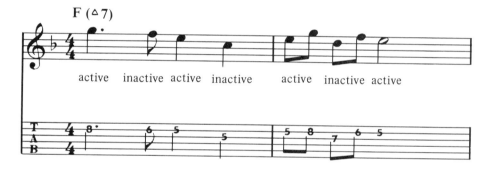

F (△7)

active   inactive active   inactive   active   inactive active

4) *Sing modal scales against a stationary chord.*

D-

Dorian

E7

Mixolydian

C△7

Lydian

5) *Play on one string.* On the guitar, unlike most instruments, there is usually more than one way to play any given note. For instance, the note C on the second string, first fret may also be played on the third string, fifth fret; the fourth string, tenth fret; the fifth string, fifteenth fret; and the sixth string, twentieth fret. If you think about it, you will realize that the only pitches that cannot be played in at least two positions are the ones found on the first four frets of the sixth string (including open E). Obviously, these duplications of notes sometimes make it difficult to find the best position for a particular melodic line. In addition, this difficulty can lock you into a style of pattern playing where your ear takes a back seat and the musicality of your lines goes right out the window. Riffs and scale patterns are good to fall back on when you don't know what else to play but they should not dictate to the higher aspect of your improvisational sense.

One surefire way to combat this problem is to begin to practice creating and mimicking melodic lines by playing on just one string. All of a sudden you are a horn player with only one fingering for that C. Furthermore, the physical difficulties imposed by playing lines on just one string force you to think more about what you are playing. No longer are you able to run with the patterns that can make your playing mechanical and unmusical.

Try getting together with another guitarist and take turns copying each other's one-string melodies. It's a challenge worth pursuing. Plus when you do go back to playing on all six strings, everything you used to do before your one-string practice experience will seem a lot easier!

Solos

On the following pages are several well-known jazz standards. The arrangements have been created to reflect the ideas covered in this book. We hope that learning and practicing these tunes will enrich your practical understanding of both the guitar and jazz.

Angel Eyes

Matt Dennis and Earl Brent

Anthropology

Dizzy Gillespie and Charlie Parker

Chords for "Anthropology"

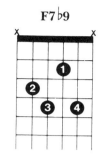
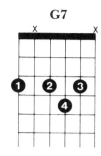

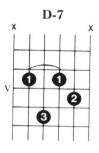
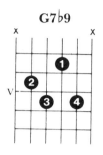
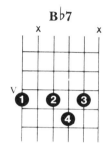
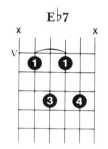
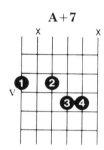

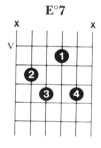
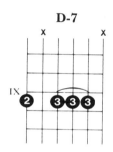
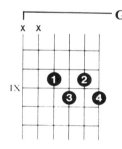
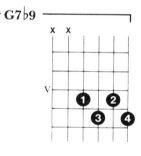
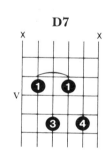

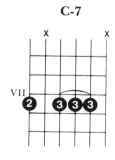
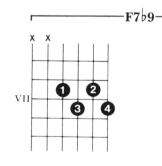
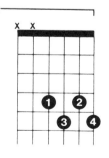
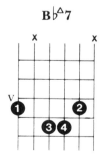
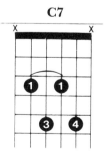

Here's That Rainy Day

Johnny Burke and James Van Heusen

You're Unique

Le Bossa qui a le cafard

Sunshine

Joe Bell

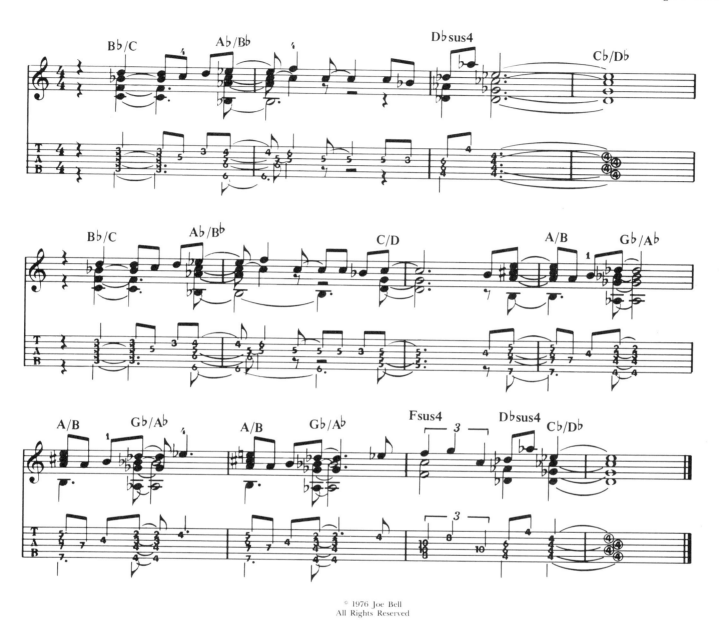

Bibliography

Books on Jazz

Aebersold, Jamey. *A New Approach to Jazz Improvisation.* New Albany, Indiana: Jamey Aebersold, 1974. This is a series of play-along records accompanied by booklets containing charts (melody and changes) for the tunes. Some of the records are devoted to the music of well-known jazz artists. These have a rhythm section playing the changes to heads of tunes made famous by the individual artist. Other records in the series are more instructional in nature covering such topics as the II V progression, the blues, jazz warm-ups, and so on. We recommend this series as extremely valuable to any beginning player. Nothing can speed up your musical development like having a professional rhythm section back you up while you try out new ideas.

Baker, David. *Jazz Improvisation.* Chicago: Maher Publications, 1969. This book can really help you put it all together—no matter what level you are at. It is a very concise and well written method book jam-packed with information for any player wishing to better understand the elements of jazz improvisation.

Coker, Jerry. *Improvising Jazz.* Englewood Cliffs, New Jersey: Prentice-Hall, Inc., 1964. This one is really fun to read. It gives a good explanation of the theory of jazz and has an outstanding glossary of chord progressions in the back.

Coker, Jerry, Jimmy Casale, Gary Campbell, and Jerry Greene. *Patterns for Jazz.* Lebanon, Indiana: Studio P.R., Inc., 1970. *Patterns for Jazz* is devoted to melodic and rhythmic patterns for different chords and scales. Although this sounds like pretty dry stuff it can help you go a long way in using scales musically and innovatively.

Ellington, Duke. *Music Is My Mistress.* Garden City, New York: Doubleday and Company, Inc., 1973. An autobiography . . .

Persichetti, Vincent. *Twentieth Century Harmony.* New York: W.W. Norton and Company, 1961. A thorough discussion of the elements of modern harmonic techniques. This is a standard reference volume at many colleges and music schools. (Persichetti is Chairman of the Composition Department at Juilliard.) Each chapter is devoted to a different harmonic technique and includes a list of recorded compositions as illustrations. It gets a bit heavy at times, and obviously much of it does not really apply to jazz, but reading through it will help you to reinforce your understanding of modern harmony in general.

Petersen, Jack. *Jazz Styles and Analysis: Guitar.* Chicago: Maher Publications (A downbeat Music Workshop Publication), 1979.

Other Books of Interest

Arban, Joseph. *Complete Conservatory Method for Trumpet.* New York: Carl Fischer Inc., 1982.

Czerny, Carl. *Art of Finger Dexterity, Op. 740.* New York: G. Schirmer Inc., 1893.

Hanon, Charles-Louis. *Virtuoso Pianist.* New York: G. Schirmer Inc., 1928.

Klose, Hyacinthe. *Celebrated Method for Clarinet.* New York: Carl Fischer Inc., 1946.

Maltz, Maxwell. *Psycho-Cybernetics.* Englewood Cliffs, New Jersey: Prentice-Hall Inc., 1960. A plastic surgeon discusses the powers of visualization and general attitude. This book can help you to achieve maximum results from your practice time, with or without your instrument.

Simandl, Franz. *New Method for the Double Bass.* New York: Carl Fischer Inc., 1964.

Thompson, Hunter. *Fear and Loathing in Las Vegas.* New York: Random House, 1971. So here is one man's version of life on the road.

Yoganada, Pavamahansa. *Autobiography of a Yogi.* Los Angeles: Self-Realization Fellowship, 1946. A great source for spiritual enlightenment. A nice book to have around for those twenty-minute breaks.

Discography

Charlie Christian
Solo Flight   Columbia G30779

Wes Montgomery
Smokin' at the Half-Note   Verve MU 2066 (reissue, import)
  (with The Winton Kelly
  Trio)
  Listen to Wes's compo-
  sition, "Four on Six."

Bumpin'   Verve V68625
                                 Polygram UMV2114

Tal Farlow
This Is Tal Farlow   Verve Clef Series MGU-8289
                                 (reissue, import)

Jim Hall and Bill Evans
Undercurrents   United Artists 14003   (both out
                                                 15003   of print)

Kenny Burrell
The Best of Kenny Burrell   Prestige 7448 (out of print)
Kenny Burrell   Blue Note 1543 (reissue, import)

Django Reinhardt
*Django Reinhardt en
  Belgione*   Polydor Special Imports
                                 2344146

Compositions, Volume 3   Inner City 1106
  (with Stephane Grap-
  pelli)

Joe Pass
The Best of Joe Pass   Pablo 2310-893

Pat Martino
Consciousness   Muse 5039
Footprints   Muse 5096

Jim Hall
The Bridge   RCA LPM 2572 (mono)   (both out
  (with Sonny Rollins)   LPS 2572 (stereo)   of print)

Various Artists
Blues and the Abstract Truth   Impulse A-95
  A good example of var-
  ious blues forms